Cowboys
America's Living Legend

CLB 1463
© 1986 Illustrations and text: Colour Library Books Ltd.,
   Guildford, Surrey, England.
Text filmsetting by Acesetters Ltd., Richmond, Surrey, England.
All rights reserved.
1986 edition published by Crescent Books, distributed by Crown Publishers, Inc.
Printed in Spain.
ISBN 0 517 61123 6
h g f e d c b a
Dep. Leg. B-12.351-86

Cowboys
America's Living Legend

Photography by
Claude Poulet

Text by
Bill Harris

CRESCENT BOOKS
NEW YORK

In February, 1907, a Hollywood producer announced that he had just come back from the Rocky Mountains with a two-reel picture called *The Girl From Montana*. Up until that point, most movies had been Vaudeville acts on film, and although there had been a few experimental "story pictures," most of Hollywood either snickered or yawned.

"It will be a pretty love story," said the press release, "typically Western in its characters and environment. In the way of adventure it promises something new and novel." More yawns. More snickers.

But in spite of what the experts thought, thousands of Americans lined up to plunk down their nickels for a look at The Girl. Before the year was over, there were similar lines for *The Life Of A Cowboy*, *The Pony Express*, and *The Cowboy And The Schoolmarm*. It was the start of an American love story, pure and simple.

Americans had been aware of cowboys long before that, of course, and they loved them right from the beginning. As the younger members of many Eastern families answered the call of the West in the early 19th century, newspaper reporters followed them and the stories they filed started a legend that hasn't stopped yet.

Operating on the theory that the real thing is worth several thousand words, not to mention dollars, the great Phineas T. Barnum imported a herd of baby bison to Boston in 1843 to provide a diversion for folks in town for the dedication of the Bunker Hill Monument. Before he sent them back to the Great Plains, he took them down to Hoboken, New Jersey, where he staged a free demonstration of Western-style calf roping. Was that P.T. Barnum who said "free"? Yes, of course, the Buffalo Roundup was free. So was the band concert that got everybody in the mood. But Hoboken is across the Hudson River from New York, and guess who controlled the ferryboat service that day.

For the next several years there was hardly a circus or a roadshow that didn't have a trick rider in a ten-gallon hat or at least a bison or two. Barnum, meanwhile, had turned his attention to other things large and small, ranging from General Tom Thumb to the wonderful Jenny Lind. It wasn't until 1860 that he looked westward again. This time his eye caught a character known as "Grizzly Adams" who had spent most of his adult life in the mountains of California capturing animals for zoos and circuses. Barnum financed an ocean voyage from San Francisco to New York for Adams and some of his beasts and introduced them to Broadway strollers with a torchlight parade. The parade included several cage wagons occupied by exotic California wildlife, but the center of attention was a platform on wheels that carried Adams and three genuine grizzly bears. Two of the bears were held in place by heavy chains, but the third was completely free to

do anything he wanted. All it seemed to want was to hear more of what Grizzly Adams was whispering into its ear. It was the first time most New Yorkers had seen anyone or anything from California. Some of their descendants haven't gotten over the impression yet. But most of all, what Adams did that night in 1860 was to fire the Eastern imagination for what would soon become known as The Wild West.

By the late 1870s, Western roundups were being staged all over the place and audiences were thrilled by the bronco busting and calf roping skills of such legendary figures as Wild Bill Hickok. But the real legend was still warming up in the wings. His name was William Frederick Cody, but he preferred to be known as just plain Buffalo Bill.

Cody had built up a reputation as a frontier scout, buffalo hunter and all-round Western character, and had traded it all in for an actor's life, playing in melodramas purported to be based on his own exploits. He didn't take much time off, but decided to go home to North Platte, Nebraska, for the big Fourth of July celebration in 1882. He was really up for it. He hadn't been back home in a long time, and the Fourth of July was a grand occasion all over 19th-century America. There was only one problem: nobody in North Platte had thought about a public celebration that year.

Cody appointed himself to stage one. Fortunately, the town had a racetrack that Bill was able to rent. He announced that it would be the site of the "Old Glory Blowout," and distributed handbills inviting local cowboys to compete for cash prizes some willing businessmen had contributed. He was able to lure a thousand entrants, not to mention their friends and families, from miles around to cheer them on. The gate receipts prompted Buffalo Bill to announce that he was planning to take the show on the road. It would be known thereafter as "Buffalo Bill's Wild West." He never called it a "show," but rather an "exhibition" of life as it existed on the American frontier. Audiences let him have it his way, but most of them knew it was a show and they loved every minute of it.

After the dust from the Old Glory Blowout had blown away, Bill went back to his touring theatrical company, but he used his time to put together a group of business partners including Doc Carver, who claimed to be the World's Champion Rifle Shot and had built a reasonably profitable traveling show he called the "Rocky Mountain and Prairie Exhibition." Together they were able to mount an all-new kind of show that played before its first paying audience in Omaha, Nebraska on May 19, 1883.

Buffalo Bill was the star of the show right from the beginning, but there were others whose names would become household words. G. William Lillie, for instance, had been hired as an interpreter for the little band of Indians who traveled with the show. Later he had a show of his own and became famous as "Pawnee Bill."

The Buffalo Bill show included such exhibitions as an attack on the Deadwood Stage, with the original stagecoach as a prop. It had a spectacular "Grand Hunt on The Plains," which included the entire cast of cowboys and Indians and assorted bison, horses, mountains goats, elk and longhorn steers. But among the great crowd-pleasers was what they called "Cow-Boy Fun;" exhibitions of roping and riding that later replaced the Wild West Show itself and became a sport known as Rodeo.

In the summer of 1883 the Buffalo Bill show went to Boston by way of Chicago, with all the important stops between. It was the event of the season at Coney Island in New York and people up and down the Eastern Seaboard were wondering if Barnum had finally met his match.

It's possible that no man in the history of the United States ever did more to enhance the glamour of the American cowboy than William F. Cody, but he was never a cowboy himself. He was born in Iowa and moved with his family to Kansas when he was eight years old. His father died when Bill was 11 and the boy got a job as a messenger carrying dispatches across the Kansas Plains. As soon as he was old enough, he became a mounted messenger for the Army after a short but glorious career as a Pony Express rider. After the Civil War he went west from Saint Louis, where he became a scout and a guide. For a brief time he contracted to supply buffalo meat for the men building the Kansas Pacific Railroad, which is where he earned his nickname.

He earned his reputation as a scout for the U.S. Cavalry when he came to the attention of General Phil Sheridan. During four years under Sheridan's command, Bill participated in no less than 16 fights with the Indians, a record for any scout. After that his position was secure as the guide of choice for visiting European dignitaries, for whom it was fashionable in the 1870s to participate in hunting expeditions out on the American prairie.

It was on one of those safaris that he met a P.R. man named Edward Zane Carroll Judson, who had found a profitable sideline in writing the mid-19th-century version of today's romance novels. They were called "dime novels" back then, and Judson was a master of the art, writing under the name "Ned Buntline." He recognized a perfect dime novel hero in Buffalo Bill, and the first story he wrote about him was so successful that Cody was invited to appear as himself in a dramatization of it on the Chicago stage.

Ned Buntline wrote three more Buffalo Bill dime novels before they parted company and Cody began writing some of them himself. By the time his Wild West moved east from Omaha in 1883 the name, if not the exploits, of Buffalo Bill were known to everyone with any adventure in their souls. The last of the books appeared in 1833. By then there were more than 1700 in print.

All the headliners in Buffalo Bill's Wild West became heroes of their own dime novel series and it all helped at the box office. But the personality that made the show the best of its kind was a little girl from Ohio who had to be seen to be believed. Her name was Phoebe Ann Moses Butler, but she preferred to be known as Annie Oakley.

No one who ever saw her ever had any serious doubts that she was the best rifle shot in the world. She hit the mark about 95 percent of the time and seemed never to miss a heart-shaped target printed on three-by-five cards that were tossed into the air at random. But even if she missed, she probably still would have been America's Sweetheart. It was said she never walked into the arena but tripped along bowing, waving and throwing kisses. By the time she began her rapid rifle fire, the audience was eating out of her hand.

Her greatest fan was the Sioux warrior Chief Sitting Bull, who joined the Buffalo Bill show in 1884 in hopes of being taken to Washington to meet the president. Even though the promise wasn't kept, he signed for a second season when he found out that "Little Miss Sure Shot" would be there with him.

Cody's itinerary was set up to allow for long runs in large cities. At the end of a six-month stand on Staten Island in New York City in 1886 he was able to move the short distance across the bay to Manhattan for a winter engagement at the new Madison Square Garden. It led to the coup of his career. Before the winter was over, he had been invited to London for the celebration of Queen Victoria's Golden Jubilee the following summer.

Though well-heeled European travelers had seen the American West and American Indians had been visiting Britain since the beginning of the 17th century, they were a little vague about American cowboys back in the Old Country. Buffalo Bill would change all that.

His entourage included some two hundred people, about half of whom were Indians. Their shipmates were two deer, ten elk, five Texas longhorns, 18 bison, 180 horses, four donkeys and ten mules.

Their first performance at Earl's Court was for the Prince of Wales, the future Edward VII, who was so enthusiastic about what he saw that he talked his mother into commanding a performance for herself. It was no easy feat. Queen Victoria had not been to a public performance of any kind since the death of her Consort, Prince Albert, nearly 26 years before. Other performances were given for other Royal figures from all over Europe, including Crown Prince Wilhelm of Germany, who took Annie Oakley back to Berlin with him. He didn't get to keep her. She and her husband rejoined the show just before they all sailed back to New York the following spring.

In the eleven months the tour lasted, their British

cousins developed a strong taste for American cowboys. The love has been kept alive in the years since by the descendants of *The Girl From Montana* who have been spreading the word in movie theaters and on television screens in every corner of the Continent.

But there were cowboys on the European Continent back when they were fighting the Hundred Years War. The whole idea was exported to America along with horses, shooting irons and even the cows themselves. The only element of the story that could be called native to North America is the Indian, one of whom was, in fact, the first American cowboy.

In 1521, the year Hernando Cortes finally convinced the Aztecs that God wanted the Spanish King to have their gold, one of the Spanish newcomers, Gregorio de Villalobos, took a look around and came up with a brilliant idea. The countryside in Mexico was very much like Western Spain, which had been a thriving cattle center for generations. Villalobos knew that explorers who had preceded Cortes had left Andalusian steers in the West Indies to fend for themselves and provide food for other Spanish explorers who might follow. On the theory that the animals would be much more at home in Mexico, he crossed the Gulf and came back with a half-dozen cows and a bull. It wasn't long before his rancho had a very substantial herd, and Villalobos bought an Aztec Indian slave to help him keep it together. The Indian's name has been lost to history, of course, but he was the first in a long line that would become an American institution. "Vaca," the Spanish word for cow, gave him the name "vaquero." "Cowboys" would come later.

The Mexican cattle industry was well-established by the time Coronado began his march through the American Southwest in 1540. He took along 150 steers to help feed his 230 mounted Conquistadores and 62 foot soldiers as well as the thousand slaves who looked after them. Though the Andalusian cattle were the toughest on earth and showed no signs of minding being led through such hostile country, they didn't move fast enough for the gold-hungry Coronado. He abandoned about half the herd in the California desert and pressed on. About 40 years later, the descendants of those 75 animals became the herds of two important ranches. One had 33,000 head, the other 42,000.

Though there were Spanish rancheros north of Mexico in the 16th century, they didn't get serious about making it an industry until about 1770, when the missionaries began moving up the California coast. The industry wasn't producing beef, but the leather of the animals' hides and the tallow of their fat, which was used to make candles and soap. The carcasses were left to rot in the sun.

The Spanish had a virtual monopoly on the cattle industry until "Anglos" began arriving in Texas in the 1820s. The newcomers weren't too interested in becoming ranchers and the unpleasantness that led to the Texas Revolution in 1835 left the hacendados free to tend their longhorns without much interference. Up until that point in the history of America, beef wasn't considered as good for food as pork, and pigs were a lot easier to handle than the ornery, wild-eyed steers who thrived in country that could only be properly called "The Great American Desert."

After the revolution, and during the years Texas was an independent Republic, the Mexican ranchers north of the Rio Grande stayed where they were and nobody seemed to care. But after Texas officially became a state in December, 1845, and war with Mexico established its southern border three years later, the Spanish-speaking ranchers were persuaded to regroup south of the Rio Grande. Most left their livestock behind.

Before the American Revolution the English colonies in the East had a cowboy culture that had been begun by Irish immigrants in the Massachusetts colony in the 1640s. Though their stock was a little less rugged than the western variety, they themselves were every bit as tough as any vaquero. Their descendants were among the thousands who flocked to the new state of Texas in the years before the Civil War. Over the years that followed, they refined the breed to make Texas beef more palatable. The Civil War, by encouraging more people to eat beef, made new markets possible. But at the same time it closed off Texas as a supplier.

Before the war, all Texas beef was shipped to New Orleans and Mobile in the coastal steamers of the Morgan Line, which completely controlled the market. When Union gunboats began patrolling the Mississippi and New Orleans fell, the Morgan boats were blockaded, leaving Texas cattle to roam and multiply. It left Texas ranchers, mostly Southern sympathizers, high and dry nursing an unrelenting hatred of the Yankees. Before the War ended, poverty in Texas was measured by the number of cattle a man owned. But, ironically, the price of livestock in Northern markets was ten times or more higher than in Texas. Hatred or no, it was tempting to get those cows up north where the money was. The great drive began in 1866, when some 260,000 head of cattle crossed the Red River into Indian Territory on the way to the railroads in Kansas and Missouri.

As much as the Texans hated Northerners, there were thousands north of Indian Territory who felt the same way about them. And they had a perfect excuse to vent their hatred. The Texas longhorn was a carrier of a tick that caused a deadly disease similar to typhoid fever in less tough cattle. In Southern Kansas and Missouri, farmers banded together and hired outlaw bands to protect their own cattle from the threat. Their actions were to prove that many of them had entirely different motives.

The cowboys who drove the herds north in the summer of 1866 left Texas with visions of riches in their heads that made any hardship worth enduring. The steers they were driving were selling for $4.50 a head in Texas and the price in Saint Louis was $40. But the trick was getting to Saint Louis. As soon as they passed out of Indian Territory they were met by armed mobs which one witness said would "...surround the driver, insult him by words such as only a cowardly bully knows how to use; spit in his face, snatch handfuls of beard from his face, tie him to a tree and whip him. In short, provoke him to a demonstration of self-defense and straightaway kill him and proceed to appropriate his herd." Others were more "civilized" in their approach. They would offer to buy the stock on the spot and pay with worthless territorial money or bad checks. Still others would wait until the cowboys made camp for the night and then stampede the herd into the darkness, where their confederates would round them up and hide them. After the cowboys had spent a day or two trying to reassemble the herd, the locals would volunteer to help, at a price. If the price proved too high for the drivers to pay, the cattle never reappeared and other cowboys drove them the rest of the way to the railroad at Sedalia, Mo.

There were other options open to Texas stockmen. The price of a steer in San Francisco, for instance, had climbed all the way to $160. There were deserts to cross on the way, though, and Apaches who didn't like thundering herds crossing their territory made the going even tougher. But none of the options made as much sense as driving cattle to the railroads crossing Kansas and Missouri. The cattle population of Texas was growing by leaps and bounds. So was the demand in the Northeast.

A young man named Joseph McCoy, who with his two brothers had built a profitable livestock business in Central Illinois, decided it was time somebody did something about the situation and elected himself to do the job. He decided it was time to relocate the rail connection point from Sedalia to some spot that would be healthier for cows and cowboys. His first stop was Junction City, Kansas, on the right-of-way of the Union Pacific. His offer to buy a tract of land for a stockyard was met first with polite laughter and then with outright hostility. He went back to Saint Louis after that for meetings with executives of the Kansas Pacific and of the Missouri Pacific. The K.P. was interested in the business potential of the idea, but not in investing any money in it. The President of the Missouri Pacific accused him of simple speculation and tossed him out of his office.

After eliminating St. Louis from his list of possible sites, McCoy took his idea to the town fathers of Solomon City and Salinas, Kansas, and in both places was hooted out of town. He finally found a small town that seemed to suit his purpose. "It was a small dead place," he said, "consisting of about one dozen log huts, four fifths of which were covered with dirt for roofing. The business of the burg was conducted in two small rooms and, of course, the inevitable saloon was to be found."

The saloon keeper spent his spare time, and he had plenty of it, raising prairie dogs that he sold to tourists passing through on their way back east from tours of the Great Plains. The town had given itself the biblical name of Abilene, and in 1867 it seemed headed for the same extinction as its namesake. But it was everything McCoy could have wanted. It was far enough west to be away from civilization and the objections that came with it. It was well-watered and offered plenty of grazing land as well as space for a stockyard that could accommodate 3000 head of cattle.

Work began on the yard, a barn with offices and a three-story hotel on July 1. Though all the materials had to be shipped in from the East, Abilene was open for business by September 5, when the first shipment went to Chicago in a 20-car train. Before the year was over 35,000 head of cattle went to market from Texas by way of Abilene.

More steers would have made the trip, but no one in Texas knew what McCoy was doing until after he had done it. He got the word out by sending a rider into Indian Territory in search of straggling herds trying to get around all the man-made obstacles they had found the previous summer. By 1868, most Texas ranchers agreed that McCoy had a good idea and, even though they didn't much like doing business with a Yankee, it was better than any of the alternatives.

It was America's first cow town, the first place America got a close look at the kind of cowboys they wrote legends about.

Of course, the Kansans didn't change their ways overnight. Before the year was over their legislature passed the "Texas Cattle Prohibitory Law," making it illegal to ship cattle from any point in the state except Ellsworth, much further east and much more vulnerable to repeats of the violence of '86. McCoy encouraged a little lawlessness in the Texans by encouraging the cattlemen to pay inflated prices for food and other supplies. Naturally, the local farmers responded with a wink and the law was never enforced.

As in the past, cattle were driven to the railroad by professional drivers, some of whom were ranchers but most of whom were entrepreneurs with a sense of adventure as well as a lust for profit. A typical driver would go from one ranch to another negotiating contracts for "beeves," which by definition were steers four years of age or better. While the ranchers were putting the number together the driver would go to horse ranches to get the horses he'd need and then he'd find cowboys to ride them.

About a third of the available men able to do the job

were either blacks or Mexicans who were more than willing to work for less than the standard $40 a month a cowboy earned in those days. But though the blacks were more likely to do work even seasoned cowboys thought was distasteful, and the Mexicans were usually better horsemen than all but the very best of them, they didn't appear on as many trail drives as post-1950s literature and films would have you believe. Most late 19th century cowboys were Civil War veterans from the Deep South who carried ideas that made the life of a black man on the trail something close to a suicide mission. The Mexican cowboys didn't fare much better. They were forced to refight the Texas war for independence several times before the drive was over.

Once the driver had his outfit together he had to go back to the cattle ranchers to gather up the stock he had bought. The contracts, usually only verbal, called for a certain number of beeves, but never specified size, shape or condition of the animals. The rancher could use a contract to get rid of anything he could round up, and though the contracts specified that steers should be at least four years old, even that rule was usually waived by custom.

The rancher was obligated to deliver the designated number of steers to a specified place where they would then become the property of the driver, who would get them to the railroad and sell them at a price he hoped would cover his costs and produce a profit. In the 1880s the routine followed a pattern that hasn't changed much in the hundred years since.

To begin fulfilling his contract, the rancher rounded up as many cattle as he could and drove them to an open spot on the prairie where a half-dozen cowboys held them together as a herd. The owner, working with one or two experienced hands, selected the animals he felt would suit the sale's requirements, but still allow him to stay in business for another year. As each was selected, it needed to be cut out from the rest, and that was when the real work began.

The cutting out process involved first quietly riding into the herd and gently nudging the selected steer to the outer edge. When it got to an appropriate spot, two cowboys working as a team dashed wildly in its direction confusing the animal which soon found itself completely separated from the rest of the herd. Its natural instinct was to get lost in the safety of the pack. But fear and confusion were, at the moment, the strongest of all instincts and by the time the animal knew what to do, it had a horse and rider at its side and another close behind. Both horses and riders knew exactly what to do.

The object of the little drama that was played out at that point was to prevent the steer from rejoining the herd. But though the ponies and men were smarter than the longhorn, the steer had strength on its side. Coupled with a generous amount of sheer terror, the animals were often downright dangerous. Their ancestors, after all, were the brave bulls who fought for their lives and made heroes of scores of Spanish matadors.

Though more closely kin to the mounted toreadors whose object was to control and not kill, the cowboy's job was not a bit less dangerous than that of anyone who ever stepped into a bull ring. But on the Texas prairie, no one was tossing roses in their direction nor shouting "olé" in admiration of their fantastic horsemanship. Often the cowboys and their quarry would run a complete circle around the herd and then do it again before the steer would finally get the message that there was a new herd forming off in the distance and it was being invited to join up.

Before the cutting out began, a small herd of oxen and cows had been set to graze a few hundred feet away from the main group. As the roundup continued, it became the destination of the cut out animals, and eventually the herd the drover would claim. When the new herd reached the required number, they were placed in a corral to wait for their new owner to come pick them up.

The drover, for whom dozens of such herds were being gathered, needed to work out a schedule of pickup that was usually a model of efficiency. His time was limited, as was the number of cowboys working for him, and there was work to be done before the drive could begin. Each of the steers, now the property of the new owner, needed to be "roadbranded," to prevent disputes along the way.

Once the drive actually began, it began almost on the run. The cattle were being led through familiar countryside, where they were likely to be inclined to take little side trips to some favorite spot. They were driven hard for a couple of other reasons, too. First of all, it got them used to the idea that they weren't free anymore. But more important, it tired them out so that when nightfall came they didn't feel much like running off. During the first few days of a cattle drive, it wasn't unusual to cover as many as thirty miles a day. Later in the drive, the average daily distance was almost never more than fifteen miles.

The drover usually had two cowboys for each 300 beeves, and each cowboy had at least two horses. The average herd, slightly more than a thousand head, traveled in an orderly column led by the drover and followed by the camp wagon and the spare horses gathered together in a herd the early cowboys called a "cavvie-yard," though it eventually became known by the Spanish name, "remuda". Together, the column would usually stretch along the trail for about three miles from beginning to end, with each steer taking the same place in line each morning after the customary two or three miles of random feeding. The steers knew the routine and followed it without much prompting. In the middle of the day they'd lie down and rest for a few hours and toward evening they'd break ranks and browse in the grass for a few miles. But for most of the time on the trail, they were as orderly as any Roman Legion, taking their cues as much from their own leaders as from the cowboys who rode beside them.

Two cowboys, known as "point men," rode at the head of the herd. The man on the right was the trail boss, usually the drover who owned the herd. His companion was the second-in-command. The next men riding beside the herd were called the "swing men," and those behind them "flank riders." The position in line was determined by experience, and those furthest forward were always the best men. "Drag riders" followed behind the herd, pushing stragglers along and looking out for strays. Needless to say, the job was as much a drag as its name, and it was usually given to kids with no experience. An even younger lad usually had the job of taking care of the horses that followed behind. Though movies usually showed the wrangler as a grizzled old fellow, the real ones who cut their teeth in 19th-century cattle drives were sometimes as young as twelve. The number of horses they had to take care of varied according to the whims and the affluence of the drover. Most outfits, especially the early ones, carried two horses per man with a few spares to cover them in case of emergency. But sometimes a drive included as many as six horses for every cowboy, which kept the wrangler on his toes.

For the most part, the cowboy's job was boring, but no trail drive was ever without its moments of heart-stopping adventure. Sometimes it could begin with a river that the lead steers decided was too deep to cross. Occasionally they made the decision in midstream, at which point they wouldn't head for either shore but just swim around in confused circles. When that happened, the trail boss was forced to ride into their midst to try frightening them into heading for the safety of dry land. He had to act quickly before too many of his charges drowned, and if he wasn't careful there was a good chance he might drown himself. It was in moments like those, when a trail boss could become unhorsed and forced to grab for a steer's tail to keep his head above the churning water, that the man in charge earned his relatively high pay of $125 a month.

The second-best job on a trail drive, in terms of salary at least, belonged to the cook. Looking back on it, though, it doesn't seem so terrific. It was the cook who gave the 3:30 A.M. signal that a new day had begun, though his own day had begun an hour before. When the herd moved out, the chuck wagon was usually already ahead of it, on the way to the next night's camp, whose site was chosen by the cook. Once having picked a spot he had to dig a pit for the fire, build it and start the day's cooking. Every day's ride was into the unknown. If there were hostile Indians or angry local farmers on the trail ahead, it was the cook who found out first.

But if his real job was to keep a cowboy's stomach from grumbling, they made sure he never heard any other kind, though they had plenty of cause to grumble. The food on a cattle drive was every bit as dull as the job itself. But, unlike the job, it didn't have even occasional excitement.

One reason why the food wasn't more sumptuous was that it had to be transported so far in a small wagon. But more important was that most of the supplies had to be waterproof. The chuck wagon was often swamped as the trail crossed deep rivers and swollen streams. And it was a rare cattle drive that didn't experience at least one violent thunderstorm that soaked everyone and everything beyond description.

Though the storms were expected, they were never welcome. "When the night is inky dark and the lurid lightning flashes its zig-zag course athwart the heavens, and the coarse thunder jars the heavens, the winds moan fresh and lively over the prairie and the electric balls dance from tip to tip of the cattle's horns – then the position of the cowboy is more trying than romantic," wrote one cowboy poet who had been there. The steers, having lived their lives on the prairie, had seen storms before and their first instinct was always to get out of its way. It didn't take much to stampede them. A crack of thunder or nearby flash of lightning was certain to do it. But something as simple as the breaking of a tree limb could get the running started.

It was in anticipation of moments like that that the cult of the singing cowboy got started. From the first day of the drive, the trail boss rode alongside the leaders of the herd repeating a short series of musical notes that helped keep them quiet and reassured. At the first sign of a stampede, he would ride to the front of the pack and calmly begin singing the familiar notes. No one who has ever been on a cattle drive doesn't believe that the wildest, most frightened of herds can't be calmed by hearing the trail boss's lullaby.

Of course, once in a while the music didn't work. It was the dread of every cowboy, but every one of them knew exactly what to do.

The only safe place to be when a herd of cattle begins to stampede is on the back of a horse. Since the 19th century cowboys were never content unless they were on their ponies, and they were usually ready the moment a stampede began. When the cattle broke into a run, so did the horses, taking their riders to the front of the column where they turned the leaders into a tight circle. The others followed and were soon calmed by the trail boss's song.

Occasionally a herd wouldn't follow its leaders, but would run off in different directions. If cowboys ever had nightmares, that was what caused them. The steers could, and often did, run as far as thirty or forty miles, and when they realized that they didn't really need to follow their leaders they became what experienced old hands called "stampeders." "Stampeding becomes a mania for them," wrote a historian, "they always seem to be looking for or studying up a pretext to set off on a forty mile jaunt."

Though the so-called stampeders represented an infinitessimal percentage of the steers in the herd, they could reduce all of their fellow-travelers to skin and bones. Once a herd was infected with them, cowboys usually responded by shooting the offenders. "The way the cowboy takes sublime pleasure (in eliminating them) is beyond expression and beggars description," said a rancher. "For he could tell you of the unnumbered sleepless nights they have cost him and how many times they have caused him to leave his couch of sweet slumber, mount his horse and ride through darkness and storm to overtake and bring back the herd from following the racy stampeders. Now that they are gone, words fail to tell his joyous delight."

Delays could make the trip from Southern Texas to Western Kansas stretch out to more than 90 days. But the trip could be made in a third of the time, though it almost never was. No one who signed up for such a journey didn't know what the adventure was going to be like. But the men who did the hiring were almost always in the dark about the men they signed up.

"We take a man here and ask no questions," said an Arizona rancher. "We know when he throws a saddle on his horse whether he understands his business or not. He may be a minister backsliding or a train robber on his vacation. We don't care. A good many of our useful men have made their mistakes. All we care about is will they stand the gaff? Will they sit sixty hours in the saddle holding a herd that's trying to stampede all the time?"

Their average age was 24. Many owned only the clothes on their backs, more often than not the remnants of the uniform and boots they were issued by Lee's army. On the trail their day began at 3:30 in the morning and they were usually in the saddle until around 9:00 in the evening after the herd was bedded down. Each man was required to serve guard duty for two hours during the night, which meant most nights they never slept for more than three hours at a stretch. Each cowboy had a saddle blanket that gave him some protection at night, though very little, and all of them covered their heads with their saddles while they were asleep. But their bed was the bare ground, some nights turned soft by driving rain. Amazingly, some cowboys lasted through as many as seven years of summer cattle drives, usually eventually retiring to their own spreads or moving to town. Though still in their early thirties, most were crippled with arthritis.

If that was the worst that happened to them, they considered themselves lucky. Though a trail driving cowboy got plenty of exercise, fresh air and sunshine, he never had fresh vegetables or eggs. Though most would probably have been horrified at what milk might do to their image, they were never offered any, not even to tame the coffee they were constantly drinking. The meat they were able to get was cooked, like everything else, over a small campfire that had been built in a pit to conserve the wood, which was hard to come by on the treeless prairie. Contrary to modern ideas about outdoor cooking, they would never dream of cooking meat over a flame because they thought the smoke, especially the smoke created by a mesquite fire, ruined the taste.

What they ate a lot of was bread, and a cook who wasn't careful might be abandoned on the trail or worse if anything happened to his sourdough starter. Before the drive began the one thing every cook was sure to do was to put some flour, salt and warm water into a covered cask. The pasty misture had to be kept warm and not allowed to get too hot or cold, which was often a serious problem. When he wanted to bake up a batch of biscuits, he filled a pan part-way with flour and dropped a handful of the starter into the center. Then he added a little salt and soda and some warm water and lard. He kneaded the mixture until it felt right, then dropped it into a greased Dutch oven which was then buried in hot coals for about half an hour. While they were baking, he was careful to add more flour, salt and water to the starter mixture so he'd be able to make more bread the next day. With pinto beans and an occasional pan-fried steak or "son-of-a-bitch stew," made from the intestines of nursing calves, mealtime on the trail was just about as dull as any other time, especially after the first month of it.

They got their excitement at the end of the trail.

Once having reached a cowtown like Abilene or Dodge City, the job wasn't quite over. A camp was made as close to town as possible, in a spot where there was plenty of water and grass for the steers to regain some of the weight they had lost on their thousand-mile trek. The cowboys had little to do but keep an eye on things and chase an occasional stray. The drover, meanwhile, went into town and checked into a hotel, which gave him a proper place to negotiate the sale of his herd. The process often took several days and herds were frequently broken up and sold to several different purchasers, which meant that there would be one final roundup to sort out which animals went to which buyer. The last roundup was the hardest for the cowboys, not because of any sentimental attachment to the cows they had been tending all summer, but because during the time the sales were being made, each of the hands had a chance to go into town to pick up supplies and have a look around.

There wasn't much to look at in an 1860s Kansas cowtown. Though some 150,000 head of cattle passed through Abilene in 1869, the town's permanent population was less than 500. Its streets were crowded at all hours, but there weren't many streets. It was doing a $3 million business in cattle, and almost as much in supplies for the men who were passing through, but there wasn't a neighborhood of mansions or fine public buildings to reflect the wealth. It was a town dedicated to the business at hand and nothing more.

But for a cowboy who had just ridden a thousand miles with a thousand cows, the business at hand was more than enough. All he wanted was to have a glass of whiskey and then another and then, who knows?

But before the drinking could begin, there was another ritual that needed to be followed. The first stop was a barber shop for a haircut and a beard trim. The next point of contact was a clothing store. Even then, no dungarees would satisfy their needs except those made in San Francisco by Levi Straus. Their new hat had to have been imported from New York and the label inside had to say "Stetson." The boots had to have stars decorating them or none of these Texans would think of wearing them. No clothing store in any cow town stayed in business long if they didn't keep up with the trends that these young men knew all about, even though they had been as out of touch as a sailor at sea for at least three months.

Once they looked presentable and smelled better than they had in weeks, they were ready for the fun to begin. "The bar-room, the theater, the gambling-room, the bawdy house, the dance house, each and all come in for their full-share of attention," reported a local observer. "In any of these places an affront or a slight, real or imaginary, is cause sufficient for him to unlimber one or more 'mountain howitzers,' invariably found strapped to his person and proceed to deal out death to such as may be in range of his pistols whether real friends or enemies. His anger and bad whiskey urge him on to deeds of blood and death."

And there were other ways a cowboy could get into trouble. The dance hall provided one of them. The contemporary observer had a word or two to say about the one at Abilene:

"The cow-boy enters the dance with a peculiar zest," he reported, "not stopping to divest himself or his sombrero, spurs or pistols, but just as he dismounts from his cow-pony, so he goes into the dance. A more odd, not to say comical, sight is not often seen than the dancing cow-boy. The front of his sombrero is lifted at an angle of fully forty-five degrees, his huge spurs jingling at every step or motion, his revolvers flapping up and down like a retreating sheep's tail. His eyes lit up with excitement, liquor and lust, he plunges in and 'hoes it down' at a terrible rate in the most approved, yet awkward country style. He often 'swings his partner' clear off the floor for an entire circle, then 'balance all' brings an occasional demoniacal yell, near akin to the war whoop of the savage Indian. All this he does entirely oblivious to the world and the balance of mankind.

"After dancing furiously, the entire 'set' is called to waltz to the bar, where the boy is required to treat his partner and, of course, himself also, which he does not hesitate to do time and again, though it costs him fifty cents each time. Yet if it cost ten times that amount he would not hesitate. The more he dances and drinks, the less common sense he will have and the more completely his animal passions will control him. Such is the manner in which the cow-boy spends his hard-earned dollars. And such is the entertainment that many young men – from the North and the South, of superior parentage and youthful advantages in life – give themselves up to, and often more, their lives are made to pay the forfeit of their sinful foolishness."

The carry-on usually lasted only a few days and often ended sooner if the cowboy's money ran out. Every fall, hundreds left Wichita and Abilene, Dodge City and Ellsworth with their pockets empty and they heads throbbing. Inevitably they headed back to Texas, where the process might start all over again the following spring. But some found better ways to use their skills as riders and ropers.

The work of most cowboys was seasonal and all of them had to find a way to keep body and soul together in the winter months when there was no work on the range or the trail. "They would not hesitate to manage a bank or a battleship if it was offered them," said one of their contemporaries. But many preferred to stay in town and try to get part-time work in local businesses. They might have earned their keep as bartenders or butchers or livery stable hands. But what most of them did most of the winter was to brag a lot about how good they were and count the days until they would have another chance to prove it.

Some were apparently right in the things they said about themselves and eventually built huge fortunes as "Cattle Barons." Consider the story of young Charlie Goodnight, who arrived in Texas from Illinois in 1850 at the age of eleven. Before he was thirteen he had taken on a herd of 430 head of cattle which he and a partner agreed to tend for the next nine years for a fee of a quarter of the calves produced each year. At the end of the first year, they had 16 calves worth $3 apiece. It was an awful beginning, but they stuck to their bargain and at the age of twenty Charlie and his partner had a herd of 4000 cattle worth $8 a head. Even split two ways, $32,000 was a nice nest egg in 1861. It was the same year the Civil War began, unfortunately, and Charlie's small herd was reduced considerably by raiding bands of Confederate soldiers. Though he had signed up to serve in the Union Army, he decided that if he was going to have a business when the War ended, he'd better get his cows out of the way first.

He drove what was left of his half of the herd across New Mexico and into Southern Colorado where he stumbled on buyers willing to buy all of them for more than double their Texas value. As soon as the deal was consummated, he went back to Texas, bought out his partner and headed back toward Colorado. But this time he wasn't as lucky. Before the herd left Texas they were attacked several times by Indians, who ran off with huge numbers of his cattle and killed several of his men.

Though he pressed on, the second sale didn't cover the first cost. But Charlie Goodnight had been poor all his life anyway, and by this point in his career he knew he had to be the best damn cowboy who ever lived. He became a professional drover and in three years earned a profit of $104,000.

During the years of the Civil War, when most cowboys and ranchers were off fighting for one side or the other, the cattle kept multiplying. It was estimated that there were close to 5 million head on the Texas range when the war ended. It left a lot of animals without any apparent owners.

Ownership of a steer was, by custom, determined by the brand of a calf's mother. In the spring each year, the hands from various ranches got together and rounded up all the local stock, coralled them, and the young unbranded animals were marked and then set free. Though the cowboys were good at finding cattle, there were always some that were overlooked. It was customary, and quite legal, for squads of cowboys to go out on the range after the formal cooperative roundup to look for some of the missing calves. Their real purpose was to find unmarked animals that legimately belonged to their employer, but they weren't always too careful to match calves with their mothers. Any calf over a year old, no matter who its mother may have been, was fair game to anyone who could get a lasso around its neck. They were known as "mauvrics," (later to be anglicized as "Maverick") for a Frenchman who went into the cattle business in Texas with a very small herd that grew very fast. He managed to get out on the range ahead of everyone else and branded an average of fifty calves for each cow he owned – for one season.

Charlie Goodnight estimated that, at the end of the War, unbranded calves outnumbered marked ones by about three to one, though he never said whether any that he drove into Colorado had relatives in other herds. But when he gave up driving for ranching in 1870, he knew enough about the ways of the West to make sure that none of his stock could ever be called a "mauvric."

Charlie settled down in Southeastern Colorado on the banks of the Arkansas River near the Eastern side of the Rocky Mountains. He had taken Texas cattle along with him, but like many ranchers in that new country, he bred them with shorthorned Durham bulls, whose ancestors had come from England. But there were differences that went beyond the characteristics of the livestock. The days of the great cattle drives were numbered. The Missouri, Kansas and Texas Railroad began pushing out from Junction City, Kansas, in 1868 and by 1873 had pushed south of the Red River to Denison, Texas. From that moment on, steers didn't have to walk to market any longer. At the same time, men like Charlie Goodnight expanded the borders of cattle country westward and northward. Their job was simply to fatten up their stock and sell at the right moment. The idea of selling steers by the head and not by the pound had passed into history too, and ranching began to become more of a profession than the seat-of-the-pants operation it had been for so long. The new country stretched all the way up to North Dakota, where the grass was thicker and greener. And though the winters were cruel, the profits waiting in the spring were guaranteed high enough to make a little frostbite no hardship at all. For the first time, ranching was more of a business than an art form, and Charlie Goodnight proved he was as good at the former as the latter.

In the early days, the cattle business was a casual affair. A drover would make a deal with a rancher and a simple letter would empower him to sell the stock at the railhead. All dealing was done on simple faith and backed by a strong code of honesty that no one would dream of violating. But in the 1870s things got more complicated. Ranchers began to specialize. Some concentrated on raising calves, others fattened them up and still others got them to market. The money that kept them all going ultimately came from Kansas and Illinois meat packers. In the meantime ranchers kept their operations going on credit. Goodnight, wearing his businessman hat, decided to get some of that action, too, and put all his assets into the banking business. It proved as disastrous as a drought. One of the recurring financial crashes of the 1870s put his bank out of business and Charlie was no better off than he had been when the Indians took the profit out of his second cattle drive.

He found his way back to Texas and on the way stumbled into the Palo Duro Canyon in the Texas Panhandle. It was in country that every aspiring rancher had long since decided was completely unfit for man or beast. But they had all overlooked the canyon, a huge tract of lush grass sheltered by its own walls which also formed a natural corral. Charlie had saved a small herd from the crash and he knew right away this was what he had saved it for. He led the herd down the steep trail into the valley and began setting up shop.

When he had the place looking presentable and the cows looking contented, he got on his horse and headed for Denver, where he knew he'd find an old friend, an Irish playboy named John Adair, who had once told him he was interested in ranching as an adventure. As one of the richest men in the West, it was no real hardship for him to give Charlie $500,000 to buy the whole canyon and stock it with 2000 of the best bulls money could buy. Within five years, Adair had all his money back, plus a profit, and Charlie Goodnight had one of the most prosperous cattle ranches the West had ever seen.

He was one of hundreds who did the same sort of thing. It was only necessary to find a running stream or water hole and settle down beside it. The government's lenient land laws allowed a man to claim all the land for miles around. The homestead ranches weren't fancy, though Charlie Goodnight used some of Adair's money to build himself a two-story log house. A budding rancher needed hired help to ride the line of the spread's outer boundaries to guard against Indians and thieves, but it didn't take much in the way of capital to become a cattle baron.

But since most of the opportunities for these men were by definition hundreds of miles from the nearest neighbor, it required a special sort of man. It was such men who devised the famous "Code of the West," which was what passed for law and order and made dime novels so popular.

The men who owned the new ranches were mostly young. Almost none was over 35. The hands who helped them were on average about ten years younger. If there was a woman within a two-day ride, she was probably the boss's wife. They all lived an impossible distance from the nearest courthouse. The lack of organized law, their young age and their isolation from women have all been cited as the reason for the problems that made the Code necessary, but there were others, not the least of which were the dime novels themselves and the general lawlessness in the entire country during the Reconstruction years. Almost no young man who drifted west in the 1860s didn't take a blood-and-thunder novel to read along the way, and very few weren't influenced by the things the novels told them everybody was doing in the West. Stealing cattle wasn't considered terribly immoral to men who had been raised in places like Georgia and Alabama, on farms that may have been taken from their families by smooth-talking judges.

The Code of the West allowed a man to take the law into his own hands and contributed mightily to the image of the American cowboy. But a good deal of it probably wasn't because of anything cowboys themselves were involved in. In 1873, the first year Dodge City, Kansas, served as a railhead for cattle drives, 25 men were gunned down in its saloons or on its streets. It was very proudly noted down in Texas that just one of the dead men was a cowboy and it surely wasn't his fault he wound up in Boot Hill. The rest of them were drifters and gamblers, probably all Yankees, too... at least that's what they said down Texas way.

In fact, it was a rare cowboy who carried a gun at all, at least after the mid-1880s when ranchers began

forbidding it. One reason was that the Code of the West made it a lynching offense to shoot an unarmed man. Being unarmed was safer most of the time. On the other hand, there were times...

The six gun, the famous "Gun That Won The West" was invented, ignominiously enough, in Paterson, New Jersey. A man named Samuel Colt was the perpetrator. Colt had done a good bit of traveling with a medicine show that introduced laughing gas to the American public. In his spare time he invented a handgun that could fire half a dozen shots without reloading. Colt wanted to become a defense contractor and made a presentation model of his gun for President Andrew Jackson. If Jackson was impressed, he didn't twist any arms in the military, and Colt's sales were limited to collectors. But Sam Colt wasn't a man to take such setbacks lying down. Though it was 1839 and the word "marketing" hadn't become fashionable yet, Sam cast his eye on the Republic of Texas, a move that would surely impress anyone today.

In the 1830s the only law and order in Texas was in the hands of the Texas Rangers, who had their hands full with a bunch of wild Indians who thought the place was theirs. Each Ranger carried a rifle, a shotgun and a single-shot pistol. When they got involved in a battle they had to get off their horses and fight on foot. The Indians, meanwhile, fought very well from the backs of their ponies. The Rangers needed the same advantage. Sam Colt liked the challenge.

He sold some repeating rifles to the Texas Navy, and when he was making the delivery he casually mentioned that he had a new weapon. Of course they were interested. The man who was most interested was a 23-year-old adventurer who had become a Captain of the Rangers. His name was Jack Hays, and he was one of the most famous Texas Rangers who ever lived. Sam Colt was part of his legend.

One day when Hays was out on patrol with a force of 14 Rangers, he was attacked by a Comanche war party. The 70 Indians were the ones who were surprised as it turned out. Hays and his men didn't get off their horses as usual, but rode right into the battle. Nearly half the Indians were killed and Hays didn't lose a single man.

Captain Jack and his men were attacked again a few weeks later. This time they were surprised while still in camp. The Rangers answered the volleys of arrows with rifle fire, but then Hays ordered his men to mount up and charge. The Comanches had never seen anything like it before. Usually the white men either looked for cover or turned and ran. These men were charging.

The Indians weren't the sort to run from a fight, so they made a stand. But these crazy white men were breaking all the rules. They kept coming, shouting and yelling and, strangest of all, spitting fire from their hands. And Indians were falling from their horses. Confused, they turned and ran. The Rangers ran after them. The chase went on for three miles before the Indians finally threw down their weapons and surrendered. Their leader said: "I will never again fight Jack Hays, who has a shot for every finger on his hand."

He actually had one more than that, but the pistol was more of a novelty than a weapon and without the element of surprise, Hays couldn't have killed many Indians with it. Though it could shoot six bullets without reloading, it had to be taken apart before the next six could be fired. It was hard to do while riding a horse and dodging Comanche arrows. The gun was also too light and not well-balanced. And worse, the bore was only .34 calibre, making it more noisy that deadly.

But it was something to build on and Sam Colt was a determined man. He took Ranger Captain Samuel Walker back to Paterson with him and the two men went to work. They made the gun bigger and stronger. They increased the bore to .44 calibre and made the grip bigger and easier to hold. They added a thick trigger guard so it could be slipped under a man's belt. And, most important, they added a rammer under the barrel so the gun could be reloaded without taking it apart. Because it was heavier, Walker said, it made a dandy club to use on people "who aren't worth shooting."

The new gun, known as the "Walker Colt," was the famous Gun That Won The West. It probably killed more men than any handgun ever made.

Actually, the gun also killed the cattle business in Abilene. From the day the first cattle drives reached there, the little town on the Kansas Prairie attracted all sorts of wicked people, gamblers and prostitutes and drifters who were considered too rough for places like Saint Louis and Kansas City, which themselves weren't exactly models of gentility. Bear River Tom Smith, the town marshal in Abilene, ordered everyone to check their guns at the city limits during the summer of 1870. But before the summer was over, someone lured him out of town and shot him.

He was replaced the following summer by James B. Hickok, known as "Wild Bill" to men who had known him variously as a buffalo hunter, a scout, a soldier, a trapper or a stagecoach driver. As the marshal in Abilene he brought a new style of law enforcement to the Wild West. Preferring to spend most of his time in the local saloon and leaving the work to his deputies, he managed to make the summer of 1871 the wildest the little town ever saw. No one violated the no-guns law, though, until near the end of the season when Wild Bill heard shots outside the saloon and rushed through the door to meet up face to face with a tough hombre named Phil Coe. Without asking questions, Wild Bill fired a shot into

Coe's stomach. Before he fell dead in the street, Coe got off two shots at the marshal, both of which missed. Meanwhile, Mike Williams, one of Hickok's deputies, rushed over to investigate. Hickok fired again and his deputy was dead. Before the sun set that day, every cowboy had left town. None ever came back as it turned out. That winter, the citizens of the county overwhelmingly agreed to sign a petition ordering Texas ranchers to take their cows elsewhere because, as the Kansans put it, "we will no longer submit to the evils of the trade."

The scene shifted to Dodge City after that, but Wild Bill drifted north, enhancing his reputation and adding notches to his gun every step of the way. Legend has it that he killed 75 men in his career as a lawman. When he accepted the job of town marshal at Deadwood in the Dakota goldfields in 1876, the drifters and gamblers swallowed hard and began wondering if there was enough gold in the Dakotas to make it worth staying.

They took up a collection among themselves and raised $300, which they gave to Crooked Nose Jack McCall, who had been selected by lot to kill the lawman.

One of the advantages of the Hickok style was that it was always easy to find him. And though McCall made it look hard, he finally downed enough whiskey to track Hickok down. The marshal was in the Number Ten Saloon, of course. He was engaged in a friendly game of poker and, fortunately, his back was to the door. One bullet to the back of the head was all it took.

McCall was captured before he could leave the saloon. He was tried by a jury of his peers and found innocent.

Neither Wild Bill nor Crooked Nose Jack was ever a cowboy. Most of the desperadoes of the old West never had the patience to endure the rather humdrum life of a cowpoke. And most of the cattlemen and their hands who left behind a record of themselves went to great pains to dispel any idea that the old West was all that wild.

One of them who had time to read the details on the 1890 Census and the mathematical inclination to figure it all out wrote: "The civilized Northeastern states have 1600 criminals to the million people while Wyoming runs 25 percent less or 1200 to the million. As a matter of fact, there is less lawlessness on the plains of the West than in any other part of the world."

Two years after the Census report was issued, the powerful Wyoming Stock Growers' Association seemed determined to take their portion of the plains of the West into the mainstream. Enraged by a highly-organized band of cattle rustlers who operated under the protection of what law there was, the cattlemen imported 20 professional gunmen from Texas. In the first skirmish of the resulting range war that became known as the Johnson County War, one of the rustlers was killed. His death prompted others of his kind from all over the West to hurry to their defense. Farmers and even some cowboys with a grudge against the cattle barons joined the fight, which became one of the bloodiest in the history of the West. The cattlemen finally prevailed on the Governor to call out the state militia, which eventually saved the gunslingers and their employers from being wiped out.

"Rustler" was a polite name for cattle thief. A combination of the words "rush" and "hustle," it was originally just another word for "roundup." Since most cattle thieves were cowboys, it was only natural that one of their own words would describe it. Stealing cattle was part of the game as far back as Spanish Colonial times, when it seemed silly to kill one of your own steers for food when someone else's were roaming the same range. As the years passed, cowboys with dreams of becoming cattle barons found the first steps enticingly simple. The cattlemen themselves weren't above bending the rules on unbranded yearlings and the men who helped them helped themselves once in a while. The vastness of the territory made it easy for a cowboy to hide a few head of cattle in a canyon or a grove of trees. And, if the ranch owner wasn't watching too closely, a good percentage of his cattle could be "cold-branded." When a piece of wet wool was put between animals and the branding iron, the brand would look just fine until the hair grew back, at which time it would disappear and the cowboy could replace it with a brand of his own.

Brands could be changed, too, of course. In the beginning they used a running iron whose curved tip could trace over a brand and alter it. Just owning a running iron eventually became a hanging offense and resourceful cowboys began getting the same effect with a piece of telegraph wire or a cinch ring.

The really determined used their long winter days, when there was nothing to do anyway, to ride out in search of calves that would be eligible for branding in the spring roundup and brand them then and there. They would either drive off or kill the mother. As long as a man didn't overdo it, his chances of getting caught were negligible. And it didn't take many steers to get a herd started.

But there were a lot of men trying. As the business began to grow in the 1870s, organizations like the Northwest Cattle Growers' Association in Texas and the Wyoming Stock Growers' Association began to put the lid on internal theft. They also made the business more efficient by settling disputes over water and grazing rights, organizing roundups and controlling diseases. They instituted brand inspectors and hired cowboys to return strays to their owners. The organizations eventually became lobbyists who made sure that the law would be forever on the cattleman's side.

They kept track of everything, even the cowboys. Unbranded orphan steers were no longer fair game, but were rounded up and sold at auctions open only to Association members. If a cowboy moved from one territory to another, the Associations saw to it that his record followed him. And if any man wanted to start a small ranch with a few head of cattle, he'd better have a bill of sale for those steers.

It all conspired to shut out small operators and encourage the big ones to get even bigger. But if they thought they had a hammerlock on the West, they were wrong.

They had opposition from more than one quarter, but the one that could provoke a stream of profanity quicker than any other was the sheepherders who had followed them out onto the plains. Any cowboy would tell you that not only do sheep eat grass right down to the roots, but they cut the roots with their sharp hooves, completely ruining cattle pastureland. What was worse, though, according to the cattlemen, was that sheep secrete an oil, the smell of which is so offensive to cattle that a steer will never walk where a sheep has been.

Besides, they argued, sheepherders did their work on foot, not on horseback, and they used dogs to do their work for them. They were clearly despicable people doing the meanest sort of work with creatures that were beneath contempt. Of course they called themselves shepherds, but no self-respecting cowboy ever did. The Biblical connotations of the word made them sound too respectable, which, of course, they were certainly not. If you were a cowboy.

A conflict between a cattle-owning family and another that ran sheep on a neighboring Arizona range led in five years to the deaths of 26 cattlemen and six herders. The war also drove out every other rancher for a hundred miles around. Up in Wyoming a band of masked men hired by the Association attacked four sheep camps at the same time one night, and after tying the shepherds to trees clubbed 8000 head of sheep to death.

The violence lasted well into the 20th century, but in the early 1870s two men walked into an Illinois hardware store with an idea that would unite the cattlemen and the sheepmen and other unlikely allies to fight a new kind of enemy. The owner of the store was John W. Gates, a man who was worth $100 million before he was fifty and was well-known all over the United States as "Bet-a-Million" Gates. What the two men showed him was a new kind of fencing material that was strong, durable and cheap. They didn't know what to do with it, but Gates did.

He took their barbed wire down to San Antonio, where he built a pen of it in the middle of town. He put 50 longhorn steers inside and then went around town betting local ranchers $100 against $10 that the steers couldn't get out. He covered more than $5000 in bets and then, just to make it more interesting, he handed a cowboy a flaming torch and told him to stampede the cattle. The fence held, the ranchers lost their bets, and Gates was in business. The West would never be the same again.

People were divided as never before. Big combines fenced in whole counties. Their neighbors came out at night and cut the fences. Small ranchers found their waterholes fenced off. Cowboys began to worry that their jobs would disappear because the wire eliminated the need for range riders. For every man who built a fence there was another man with a pair of wire cutters. And chances were good that each of them had a gun.

In the years before the wire began appearing, cattlemen had been irritated by whole families of what they called "nesters." They called themselves "homesteaders," and backed up their rights to farm the prairie by a federal law that encouraged it. Cowboys didn't bring out the welcome mat for them. For one thing, they broke up grazing land. But worse, they represented a different way of living, and to freedom-loving cowboys and stockmen, it was clearly a threat. It went beyond the simple matter that sod-busters were digging up valuable pasture land. These new people had wives and that meant children and that meant schools. Next thing a man knew, they were building churches. It cut to the very core of a cowboy's self-image.

Eventually, of course, the nesters' girl children grew up and the next generation of cowboys began thinking about marriage in a different way. But nothing brought the two groups together more than "bob-wehr." Both stockmen and farmers had a love-hate relationship with the stuff. Sometimes it was a blessing, sometimes it just got in the way. In the end, of course, the wire won. But there were days out there when you couldn't get good odds on it.

The fences made it easier to own land and know just what you owned. They made it easier to keep cattle where you wanted them and they made it possible to breed better, more profitable strains. And cowboys who had worried that fences would make the range rider a thing of the past simply changed the job description to "fence rider" and kept on riding.

If anyone is still alive who remembers the 19th century cowboys, whose Golden Age ended in the 1880s, God bless 'em. But most of us have to rely on what we've read or seen in the movies. Yet there is no other character in American history that so many Americans have fixed so firmly in their minds. It's inconceivable that there was ever a fat cowboy, for instance. And if any had beards, they were probably up to no good. Though we know they led violent lives and many carried guns, we never think of a cowboy with scars or missing limbs. It's obvious that their diet left many of them victim to such diseases as scurvy, but when's the last time you ever thought about a cowboy getting sick?

One of the earliest descriptions that may have set the pace for the future was written in 1874 by Joseph McCoy, the Illinois man who established the cattle market at Abilene.

"They are, as a class, not liberally educated," he said, "and but few of them are extensive readers. But they are possessed of strong natural sense, well skilled in judging human nature. They are close observers of all events passing before them, thoroughly drilled in the customs of frontier life, more clannish than the Scotch, more suspicious than need be, yet often easily gulled by promises of large prices for their stock. They are very prone to put an erroneous construction upon the acts of a Northern man and inclined to sympathize with one from their own state as against another from the North, no matter what the Southern man may have been guilty of. To beat a Northern man in a business transaction is perfectly legitimate, for they regard all such as their natural enemies of whom nothing good is to be expected.

"Nothing arouses their suspicions to a greater extent than a disinterested act of kindness. They are fond of a practical joke, always pleased with a good story and not offended if it is of an immoral character. They are universal tipplers, but seldom drunkards. They are cosmopolitan in their loves, but always chivalrously courteous to a modest lady. They possess a strong innate sense of right and wrong and a quick, impulsive temper. They are great lovers of a horse and always good riders and good horsemen. They are always free to spend their money lavishly for such objects or purposes as best pleases them. They are very quick to detect an injury or insult and not slow to avenge it nor quick to forget it. They are always ready to help a comrade out of a scrape. They are full of life and fun and would brook the rules of restraint, free and easy."

Though he was fairly sure none of them would read what he had written and his description probably wouldn't have offended any cowboy or cattleman, McCoy had to do business with these people, and he was a damn Yankee after all. A few paragraphs later in his history, he softened what he had said:

"They had just passed through a bitter civil war, which graduated their former education of hatred and suspicion of Northern men. And above all, the long and bitter experiences they had endured in Southern Kansas and Missouri: swindling, outrage, robbery, rapine and murder were sufficient to embitter beings more than human."

In 1888 Theodore Roosevelt, who had his first taste of politics two years before, advanced the image a little further in the direction of pure romance. He hadn't noticed that cowboys didn't read much, nor that they weren't famous for voting in national elections. His account of his life in the Dakotas said of his neighbors:

"To appreciate properly his fine manly qualities, the wild rough rider of the plains should be seen in his own home. There he passes his days, there he does his life work, there, when he meets his death, he faces it as he has faced many other evils, with quiet, uncomplaining fortitude. Brave, hospitable, hardy and adventurous, he is the grim pioneer of our race. He prepares the way for civilization before whose face he himself must disappear."

T.R. was one of hundreds of "dudes" who went west in the early 1880s. Several of his Harvard classmates were already ranching in the Dakotas when he first went there in 1883 to add buffalo hunting to his list of accomplishments. A year later he joined them again and established a ranch of his own in the Badlands. The land itself was free for the taking, but he put more than a quarter of his personal fortune into the outfit, which he stocked with nearly 5000 head of choice cattle.

His own image of a ranch owner was slightly different from the men of a decade before who were called cattle barons, but lived as crudely and worked as long and hard as any man who worked for them. Roosevelt said that his peers "show more kinship to an Arab sheik than to a sleek city tradesman." He saw them as men with plenty of time for good books and hunting expeditions. "It was a life closely akin to that of the old Southern planters," he said. It was significant that the two books he wrote about his experiences in the Wild West were each fancy editions that sold for $15 in that era of dime novels.

The future president was a bully good sport who loved the West with all the passion at his command. Once, after seven days of trailing a buffalo herd all the way to Montana, he turned to his companion and said "By Godfrey, this is fun!" and, though they had to stifle a laugh, everybody knew he was probably the happiest man alive. He tried to be a cowboy, too, but his heart was stronger than his body and if he hadn't been the boss, the cowboys on his own ranch probably would have run him off the place in a general easterly direction. Behind his back they called him "four-eyes." There wasn't a cowboy for hundreds of miles around who hadn't heard about the time Mr. Roosevelt began a cattle drive by shouting to the foreman, "Hasten quickly there!" but none of them had not also retold the story over and over of the night in a Montana saloon when a drunken cowboy armed with a pair of sixguns decided it would be fun to make fun of the puny dude. T.R. didn't take a minute of it, but marched up and flattened him with a single punch.

They liked his personal style, respected his firmness and admired his fairness. But what they liked most about Teddy Roosevelt was the style of his clothes. His boots were custom-made of alligator skin and his Bowie knife was custom-mounted in silver by Tiffany of New York. His buckskin shirts were tailor-made, as were his buckskin suits. His belt buckle and his spurs were made of pure silver, the belt was engraved with a bear's head, the spurs with his initials. But the thing the cowboys envied most was his Colt sixshooter. The barrel was engraved and plated in both silver and gold. The handles were genuine ivory, embossed on one side with the head of a buffalo and on the other with his initials.

If they had nothing else in common, 19th century cowboys enjoyed dressing well. Granville Stuart, a rancher who recorded life in Montana in the '60s and '70s, wrote of the men who worked for him:

"They wore the best clothes they could buy and took great pride in their personal appearance and in their trapping. The men of our outfit used to pay $25 a pair for made-to-order riding boots when the best store boots in Helena were $10 a pair. Their trappings consisted of a fine saddle, a silver-mounted bridle, pearl-handled sixshooter, latest model cartridge belt with a silver buckle, silver spurs, a fancy quirt with silver mountings, a fine riata sometimes made of rawhide, a pair of leather chaps and a fancy hatband often made from the dressed skin of a diamond rattlesnake. They wore expensive stiff-brimmed light felt hats with a brilliantly colored handkerchief knotted about their necks, light colored shirts and exquisitely fitted high heeled riding boots."

Stuart comes close to the common perception the rest of us carry in our hearts about these knights of the prairie. Walter Prescott Webb, a more recent historian, came even closer when he wrote:

"He swears like a trooper, drinks like a fish, wears clothes like an actor and fights like the devil. He is gracious to ladies, reserved toward strangers, generous to his friends and brutal to his enemies."

Even though there is a common thread that runs through nearly every contemporary account and historian's analysis, the description of the American cowboy that has influenced each and every one of us and has given us the perception we all believe, was this one, written in 1902:

"Lounging there at ease against the wall was a slim young giant, more beautiful than pictures. His broad, soft hat was pushed back; a loose-knotted, dull scarlet handkerchief sagged from his throat, and one casual thumb was hooked in the cartridge belt that slanted across his hips. He had plainly come many miles from somewhere across the vast horizon, and the dust upon him showed. His boots were white with it. His overalls were gray with it. The weather-beaten bloom on his face shone through it duskily, as ripe peaches look upon their trees in a dry season. But no dinginess of travel or shabbiness of attire could tarnish the splendor that radiated from his youth and strength."

He was known simply as *The Virginian*, the creation of Owen Wister, whose narrator told his readers that his first impression of the man was from a passing train:

"For the first time I noticed a man who sat on the high gate of the corral... For he now climbed down with the undulations of a tiger, smooth and easy, as if his muscles flowed beneath his skin. The others had all visibly whirled the rope, some of them even shoulder high. I did not see his arm lift or move. He appeared to hold the rope down low by his leg. But like a sudden snake I saw the noose go out its length and fall straight and true; and the thing was done. As the captured pony walked in with a sweet church-door expression, our train moved slowly on to the station and a passenger remarked: 'That man knows his business'."

Though scholars have spent the rest of the century analyzing Wister's novel as a political parable, most Americans accepted it as a good read, and by 1929, when the second movie based on it was released, Gary Cooper fitted the image so perfectly he was able to play the title role wearing a black hat.

The film, one of the early talking pictures, also cemented into everyone's consciousness the most famous line from the book. When the villain, Trampas, played in 1929 by Walter Huston, found his stomach at the business end of the Virginian's sixshooter during a dispute over a game of poker, he gave the performance of his career after being cautioned, "When you call me that, smile!" He smiled a Walter Huston smile.

The last of the four filmed versions of the book, starring Joel McCrea, came along in 1946. Brian Donlevy was the one who was warned that time. A reviewer said he was "conventionally dark and dirty," but dismissed the whole affair as "pedestrian." Too bad. They had a lot of tradition on their side.

Like his friend Theodore Roosevelt, Owen Wister was a Harvard man. He had early dreams of being a musician, and on the obligatory Grand Tour of Europe after his graduation in 1882, he had a private audience with Franz Liszt, who listened to one of the young man's compositions and told him that he had a "pronounced talent."

But he didn't like Europe, where a musical career would surely have taken him, and opted to go back to New England, where he dabbled in the direction of a career in banking and then in teaching. Nothing suited him and he finally wandered west for what was known as a "rest cure," and fell in love with the people and the countryside of Wyoming. In his first blush of enthusiasm in the summer of 1885, he wrote:

"We Atlantic Coast people, all varnished with Europe and some of us having a good lot of Europe in our marrow besides, will vanish from the face of the earth. We're no type, no race, we're transient... All the patriotism of the war doesn't make us an institution yet, but the West is going to do it."

Four years before, a former Yale football player also went West. He said of his first experience in Montana:

"I knew the wild riders and the vacant land were about to vanish forever, and the more I considered the subject, the bigger the forever loomed. Without knowing exactly how to do it, I began to try to record some of the facts around me, and the more I looked, the more the panorama unfolded. I saw the living, breathing end of three American centuries of smoke and dust and sweat."

His name was Frederic Remington. But it wasn't until 1884, after having run a mule ranch in Kansas, that he went down to Arizona and found out exactly how to record the facts around him. His paintings, drawings and sculptures constitute one of the best records we have.

He did his first paintings in Arizona during the summer of 1884 and found a market for them among saloon-keepers looking for something to decorate their barrooms. He made $250 and decided it was an artists' life for him.

As happens in the life of every artist, the going was tough at first. Then, in 1895, the famous Apache, Geronimo, cut loose from the Reservation and was getting a lot of attention for himself with his escapades in Arizona. It was big news back East. But though newspapers had no trouble finding words to describe what was going on, their readers had no idea what this "Arizona" looked like. They needed pictures and Remington had lots of them. The only problem was that his pictures showed cowboys and soldiers, Indians and horses in action. They could have been sketched anywhere. In fact, most of the work that went back East that year had been done in Wyoming.

But it made people notice Frederic Remington, and among the men who were impressed was Owen Wister.

They eventually became collaborators, supplying stories and art to magazines like *Harper's Weekly*. For nearly ten years, neither Remington nor Wister did any work at all that didn't involve the other. They saw the West through each other's eyes and shared the vision with the world. Then one day a neighbor watching him work was amazed at the ease with which Remington was able to remove a figure and completely turn it around. "You're not a draftsman, you're a sculptor," he said, and Remington's mind began turning.

It was a while before the message got through, but in October, 1895, *Harper's* was obliged to run a Remington photograph rather than a Remington drawing. It was a picture of a bronze sculpture called *The Bronco-Buster*. "For the first time," said the magazine's art critic, "we see the cowboy as he really is, divested of the nonsense of romance... The serious fight between man and horse is given with a realism and intensity that comes only from profound knowledge.

Remington and Wister continued working together after that, though by the time *The Virginian* was published, Remington was working exclusively for *Collier's* magazine, and the book appeared without any artwork. But at about the same time Remington was putting the final touches on his *Bronco-Buster*, he produced a painting called *The Last Cavalier*, which Wister said "will haunt me forever." The picture, one of the illustrations for Wister's *The Evolution of The Cow-Puncher* "should be set to music," he said.

Wister's "Evolution" was considered in 1895 to be the final word on the subject. It ended, in fact, with a sort of epitaph:

"And what has become of them? Where has this last outcropping of the Saxon gone? Except where he lingers in the mountains of New Mexico he has been dispersed, as the elk, as the buffalo, as all wild animals must inevitably be dispersed. Three things swept him away... the exhausting of the virgin pastures, the coming of the wire fence, and Mr. Armour of Chicago, who set the price of beef to suit himself. But all this may be summed up in the word Progress. When the bankrupt cow-puncher felt Progress dispersing him, he seized whatever plank floated nearest him in the wreck. He went to town for a job; he got a position on the railroad; he set up a saloon; he married and fenced-in a little farm. And he turned "rustler" and stole the cattle from the men for whom he had once worked. In these capacities you will find him today.

"The ex-cowboy who set himself to some new way of wage-earning is all over the West, and his old courage and frankness still stick to him, but his peculiar independence is of necessity dimmed. The only man who has retained that wholly is the outlaw, the horse and cattle thief, on whose grim face hostility to Progress forever sits. He has had a checkered career. He has been often hanged, often shot; he is generally 'wanted' in several widely-scattered districts... This stripe of gentleman still lives and thrives, occasionally goes out into the waste of land in the most delicate way, and presently cows and steers are missed. But he has driven them many miles to avoid livestock inspectors, and it may be that if you know him by sight and happen to be in a town such as Kansas City where cattle are bought, you will meet him at the best hotel there, full of gentility and affluence.

"Such is the story of the cow-puncher, the American descendant of Saxon ancestors, who for thirty years flourished upon our part of the earth and because he was not compatible with Progress, is now departed, never to return. But because Progress has just now given us the Populist and silver in exchange for him, there is no ground for lament. He has never made a good citizen, but only a good soldier, from his tournament days on down."

Of course, the news of his death was premature.

Though the life of a cowboy changed before the end of the century, life went on. And his "tournament days" continue to this day in a thing they once called "Cow-Boy Fun," but now call "Rodeo." Though the word itself is Spanish, the sport is decidedly American. And quite possibly the wildest, most dangerous on the face of the earth.

The sport is as old as the institution. Even Spanish vaqueros succumbed to it. In the beginning it was connected with the roundup, which the Spanish called a rodeo. It was the only chance range cowboys got to see men from other outfits, and few could resist the chance to do some showing-off. In Spanish California, one of the ways they did it was to bury a chicken so that only its head was exposed and then see who was skillful enough on the back of a horse to decapitate the poor thing at a full gallop. Fortunately, that event has not come down to us as a standard rodeo feature.

Most of the events that have are job related. In early roundups they competed for nothing more than the glory that comes with being the best man in the outfit, which every cowboy was convinced he was. The sport got a sort of professional status in the 1880s when Buffalo Bill and others took the show back East. It represented a good opportunity for off-season employment, and many who took advantage of it never went back to the real thing. They were known as "rodeo cowboys," and it didn't take them long to wear out their welcome in the cities they visited. Cities began to ban them because, as one editorialist said: "As a class, they are foulmouthed, blasphemous, drunken, lecherous and utterly corrupt. Usually harmless on the plains when sober, they are dreaded in towns."

But the sport survived both the alleged perpetrators and the critics. People enjoyed watching them. The mid-1880s marked the high point of outdoor shows in America. There were more than 50 circuses on the road bringing fame to such men as James A. Bailey, W.W. Cole, Adam Forepaugh, the Sells Brothers and the Ringling Brothers. Most of them saw the box office value of having some cowboys along, no matter what the editorials said about them.

A dozen or more Wild West shows, all competing for the same half-dollar ticket price, constituted part of the reason, but there was another. The Cow-Boy Fun segment that had become the most popular part of every Wild West was becoming serious competition in the Western states, where local cowboys were saving their hard-earned dollars to pay entry fees in local competitions for cash prizes. The annual events were generally called "Stampedes" or "Round-Ups." One of the first was the Cheyenne, Wyoming, Frontier Days, which began in 1897. Others followed, including the Pendleton, Oregon, Round-Up, dating back to 1910 and the Calgary, Alberta, Victory Stampede, which was first held in 1919.

In the years following World War I, before the name Rodeo caught on, the idea began to spread across the country. The New York Stampede at Coney Island in 1916 may have started it all, but Buffalo Bill staged one in Chicago the same year. In 1925, a promoter named Tex Austin leased Chicago's Soldier Field and put on the first "World's Championship Rodeo," which became the Chicago Rodeo and made money for competing cowpokes and for Mr. Austin for the following three years. The designation "World's Championship" went to New York in 1926 with an annual show at Madison Square Garden and to Boston Garden in 1932. Both ran for many years and both called themselves the world's championship event. Nobody seemed to care much about the contradiction, least of all the promoter who staged both events.

He was Colonel Bill Johnson. He had gone east from Texas and turned his roots into a very profitable enterprise. The cowboys who followed him were easily the best of their breed, but their share of the profits didn't make many of them rich. It had been established in local competitions that participants were responsible for all their own expenses as well as entry fees. The Boston Rodeo always followed the New York show and as a rule attracted the same participants. Together, that represented about a month of time, during which a cowboy was forced to stay in a hotel since both Boston and New York each had rules against sleeping on their streets. In most cases, they had a pony to board, which, added to the cost of getting them both all the way across the country in the first place, made competing an expensive proposition.

But the purses were big, too, and a good man could earn a good bit more money than the schoolmarm back home and have more fun doing it. Many came away with nothing, of course, it was a competition, after all.

By 1936, the competitors decided they'd had enough. After tickets went on sale for the Boston Garden event, more than 50 of the top hands circulated a petition demanding that prize money should be doubled for each event and that the winner of each would, in addition, have his entrance fee refunded. The petition ended with the ominous warning: "Any cowboy failing to sign this Petition will not be permitted to contest, by order of the undersigned."

It was a strike. Johnson put on a show anyway, but it was no crowd-pleaser and he had already sold tickets for ten more days of the same thing. The next day he capitulated and increased the prize money, but he also made the cowboys sign a no-strike agreement that was binding on "heirs, next of kin and assigns."

A month later, the cowboys formed a union. They all agreed that the idea had been painfully slow in coming, and decided to name their new organization the *Cowboys Turtle Association*. They put teeth in their turtle by stipulating that any cowboy competing in a rodeo the CTA hadn't approved would be forced to pay a $500 fine. They also promised a $100 penalty to anyone guilty of bad conduct. It was a big step for these apostles of rugged individualism, but they all agreed that the time had come to bite the bullet.

But they also bit the hand that could feed them. Their high-handed threats resulted the following year in the Pendleton Round-Up's edict that "no turtles need apply." The show required that all participants had to be amateurs, working cowboys and not professional rodeo contestants. Other Western competitions followed the lead.

The big Eastern competitions didn't have a pool of amateurs to draw on, though, and the East was still where the big purses were. The Turtles prevailed and eventually became less strident, and it was generally agreed that the sport needed a few rules, even though the people on both sides were pretty mulish individuals.

They must have been doing something right. The popularity of the sport grew by leaps and bounds in the '30s, and though newspapers doggedly refused to cover it as a sport, there were no cowboys anywhere who understood why. They did get a certain amount of satisfaction that sportswriters gave a lot of space to a new class in major horse shows, the quarter horse. It was the same animal cowboys had been depending on for 200 years.

By 1940, amateur rodeos had become almost a thing of the past. People who paid to watch the competitions preferred the professionals who trained for their specialties as hard as any professional athlete and fought hard to win because they wouldn't get paid if they didn't. "If every sport operated under rules like these," said one cowboy, "there wouldn't be as many sports."

Though a great many rodeo cowboys signed up to help fight World War II, the sport became even more popular during the war years. As an all-American contest, it stirred more than its share of patriotism. And in spite of the fact that most of the established annual contests shut down "for the duration," cowboys in uniform put on shows at military bases and enlisted new, enthusiastic supporters.

When the war was over and colleges began filling up, rodeo became a college sport in many Western states and that, more than the open range, is where most of today's contestants have cut their teeth.

The rewards are better, too. A bronc rider may not earn as much as a baseball outfielder, but in 1976 Tom Ferguson of Oklahoma became the first cowboy to win more than $100,000 in rodeo competition, and there have been many who have followed in his footsteps. But for every big money winner, there are dozens who come away with just a belt buckle or a watch.

Whatever they get they earn. Take bareback riding, for instance. Of all the rodeo events, it's the fastest and most popular with the audiences. It goes back to the days when there wasn't a cowboy alive who didn't believe that he could ride even the spookiest pony and show him who's boss. And though they probably proved it time and again on horse ranches, it didn't become a standard rodeo event until about 1926.

The rules are simple. It's the event that's hard. The horse is equipped with a ten-inch leather cinch that has a handle on top. The cowboy is equipped with mothing more than strength and experience. He has no way of controlling the horse and according to the rules can't hang on with more than one hand. He can't switch hands either, nor touch the horse in any way. His free hand has to wave in the air. The rider mounts the horse through a chute and must spur at the first contact. If he misses, he loses. The rider has to keep on spurring the animal as long as he stays up. The spurs themselves are dull, but the horse gets the message and does all it can to get rid of the man on its back. The ride is limited to eight seconds, a rule based on the theory that a man can get a feel for a bronc in ten and improve his own chances.

The only rule that favors the rider is that if he is thrown as he leaves the chute or if the horse falls down, he gets a second chance with a different animal. If he stays for the eight seconds or if he's thrown before that, a team of mounted pick-up men get him out of the way. But mostly a bronc rider hopes for a soft landing well away from the horse's hooves.

If you think that riding a saddled bronc is easier, guess again. The horse in this case has a plain halter with a rein tied to it. If the horse bucks with its head high, the rein needs to be short, if he bucks low, the rider needs to hold the rein further back. He's allowed to use only one hand, and if he makes a mistake in judgement, he not only gets thrown, but scores zero points. He gets zero points if one of his feet leaves a stirrup, too. But if he's thrown, both feet better leave the stirrups or he's in big trouble.

Like the aerialist act in a circus, or the boomers that end a fireworks display, the climax of every rodeo is the riding of brahma bulls. It's an event that goes back to the days when cowboys were sure they could ride anything that had four legs, and is not far removed from the Spanish bullfight. But in this case, the man doesn't try to kill the bull. He's too busy trying to keep from being killed himself. A cowboy on a buckinng bronco is sure that once the horse has gotten rid of him, it will walk away with no thoughts of revenge. But bulls are a different sort of animal. Once they've thrown their rider, they're likely to turn and fight. The pick-up men who rescue bronc riders are useless because the bulls attack them, too.

All that can be done is to distract the beast until the rider can pick himself up and run for cover. That job belongs to clowns who dress and often behave like their cousins in the circus, but have a much more serious job to do.

They work in pairs, one on foot, the other in a padded barrel. The walking member of the team is a direct descendant of the matadors. It is his job to get in front of the bull and distract him. But the bull, though easily distracted, is faster and has more stamina than the man, and that's where the guy in the barrel comes in. All the bull wants to do is hit something, and the moving barrel is a terrific target. They look funny, and are great crowd-pleasers, but without them we'd surely have a lot fewer cowboys to cheer on.

The man riding the bull has enough problems. The rigging he uses is a knotted piece of rope that can be pulled tight but instantly released. It has a double braid at the top that the rider wraps around his hand, and, as is the case with bronco riding, he can use only one hand. The rope has a bell fastened beneath it to give the bull something extra to get mad about and to add weight to the rope so it will fall free when the rider does. The bull also wears a flank strap, a broad leather belt that's tightened just enough to make the animal want to get rid of it.

Time for the event is the same as for bronco riding, just eight seconds. It takes an exceptional man to last as long as that. But most people who compete in rodeos are exceptional. They are all heirs to a proud tradition.

Though riding bulls was never part of a cowboy's job, grabbing a 700-pound steer by the horns and wrestling him to the ground often is. In competition it usually happens so fast that it looks easy. It isn't. The steer, which has been chosen by lot, comes running from a chute and once it has passed a pre-marked score line horse and rider rush up behind and then beside it. When the dogger decides he's reached the right spot, he slides from the saddle onto the steer's neck. The momentum throws his feet forward, and as he hits the ground, he digs in his heels. Then all he has to do is grab the steer by the horns, push on one and pull on the other and throw the animal off balance. The steer has to go down in exactly the right way or it doesn't count. The rules say it has to be lying on its side with all four feet extended and the head straight. It's a timed event that a champion steer wrestler can do in four or five seconds. Obviously, it often takes a bit longer.

The relationship between a cowboy and his horse is less critical in steer wrestling than in calf roping, a rodeo event some purists say really takes you back to the days of the open range, when a man and his horse were a magnificent team.

The pony is already working before the dogie comes running out of the chute. They need to start running after it at precisely the right moment and the horse needs to get up to top speed in a couple of yards and then be ready to stop on a dime the instant the rider tosses the loop over the calf's head and pulls the rope tight. At that moment, the rider is himself running toward the calf, which he will have to throw to the ground. Once he's done that, he has to take the piece of twine he's been carrying in his mouth and wrap it around the calf's foreleg. Then he grabs the hind legs, pulls them forward, and with three quick wraps ties them all together. Mr. calf, meanwhile, isn't taking all this lying down. There's a whole lot of squirming going on. But through it all, the cow pony, acting independently, holds his ground and keeps the rope tight.

Sometimes the person knocking over that 200-pound calf isn't a man, but a woman. It isn't even uncommon. But what would they have thought of cowgirls back at the turn of the century?

They loved them, of course.

In 1900, the *New York World* wrote of a 14-year old girl "...who weighs only 90 pounds, can break a bronco, lasso and brand a steer and shoot a coyote at 500 yards. She can also play Chopin, quote Browning, construe Virgil and make mayonnaise dressing. She is a little ashamed of these latter accomplishments, which are a concession to the civilized prejudices of her mother."

Will Rogers, who appeared with her in a traveling show the following year and took second billing, claimed that he had coined the word "cowgirl" especially for this young woman, whose name was Lucille Mulhall. He didn't mention that her sisters Bessie and Georgia were also riders and ropers in the same show and every bit as deserving of the new name. But Lucille was something special.

Foghorn Clancy, who traveled the rodeo circuit for fifty years as a cowhand and announcer, wrote about the first time he saw her at Oklahoma City in 1902.

"Colonel Zack Mulhall had imported from Saint Louis a cowboy band of about 30 musicians. I don't suppose they were real range hands, but they dressed in full cowboy regalia... boots and spurs and all. Each carried a holstered sixshooter. There were several selections they played where at certain points they all drew their sixguns and fired them off in unison. This may not have been music, but it certainly was loud, and in the lobby of the hotel the effect was something like that of an earthquake.

"The day before the contest was to open, there was a grand parade down the main street, which wasn't paved in those days. Cowboys and cattlemen from all over the territory rode on prancing ponies. The cowboy band played and fired their guns. Banners waved, ponies danced, kercheifs waved, lariats swished and cowboys yelled, jingled their spurs and made merry.

"Several times along the line of march, a slender girl broke from the line of riders and sent her pony onto the sidewalk and right into a bank. She would ride up to the cashier's window and leaning from the saddle, present a check to be cashed.

"This amazing girl was Lucille Mulhall, then only about seventeen years old, but destined to make history in rodeo... The big feature of this rodeo was steer roping, and Lucille was better at it than most men. She had the dash and daring of a man twice her size and she never hesitated to tie onto the biggest and wildest steer. She had the knack of throwing her trip rope over and really giving the longhorn a 'fairground bust,' that is, she threw them so hard that they seldom got up before she could tie them.

"Lucille was a born cowgirl, having been reared on a ranch with a lariat in her hands from infancy. Once, while still in her early teens, during a visit of Theodore Roosevelt to Oklahoma, she roped a coyote from horseback and after giving it a couple of hard bumps with her lariat, leaped from the saddle and finished the animal with one blow of her iron-handled quirt. Roosevelt was amazed and proclaimed it was the greatest stunt he had ever seen a girl perform."

She worked in her family's Wild West show, where she dazzled audiences with a stunt that involved roping six running horses at the same time. Though Annie Oakley had preceded her in making a statement about a woman's place in the Wild West, Lucille was the first to do all the things that before her time had been considered jobs for men only.

In spite of the fact that women invaded their turf earlier than a great many other professions, the world of a cowpoke is still very much a man's world. But that's far from the only tradition that still lives. The language, with its origins in 18th-century Spanish California, is still the same. Though they don't make them of rawhide like their vaquero ancestors did, every cowboy still works hard to be the best at handling "la reata," which he calls a lariat. Their saddles bear a strong resemblance to the Spanish war saddles that Coronado's men took into the Southwest, and when they rope a steer, they hold him in place by taking quick turns around the saddle horn. Their ancestors called that "dar la vuelta," they call it dallying. The pommel itself came to the Spanish from the Moors, who invented it to keep a lance-wielding soldier from falling off his horse.

The cowboy's most important tool, his horse, also has a Moorish background. They went to Spain from North Africa and eventually to Mexico with Cortes. Over the years, strays, which the Spanish called "mesteño," reproduced on the open range and became fair game for any cowboy with the skill to catch one. The cowboy called his prize a mustang. Traditionally, they roamed free for the first four years of their lives, then were rounded up and corraled. The next step was to "bust" them, a process that took about four days and often took as much out of a man as a pony. The basic idea was to domesticate the wild animal. Usually every outfit had a specialist who worked with a "class" of six or eight at a time. First he'd rope the animal and tie it to a fence post while he put on a bridle. Once the mustang got used to that idea, the cowboy tossed a blanket on his back and then hoisted a 40-pound saddle over it, an operation that had to be done with one hand since no mustang ever held still for that kind of treatment and the man was obliged to keep a firm hand on the rope or risk being trampled.

The next step was for the cowboy to climb aboard himself and with spurs and quirt to show the animal who was boss, all the while hanging on for dear life. The training process was something a horse never forgot, nor ever wanted to go back to, and it was probably the only time in the relationship of a cowboy and his horse that could come close to being called cruel treatment. No matter what they did to each other, there isn't a cowboy who ever lived who wasn't proud of the animal who shared his job and on whom his life often depended. Cowboys considered walking beneath their dignity, and some even stayed mounted when they dropped in at cowtown saloons, which may be where Mulhall got the idea for her banking stunt in Oklahoma City.

The cowboy's traditional boots, which evolved from the boots they wore in the Civil War, got narrower in the evolutionary process because cowboys claimed they wanted a "snug fit." What they really wanted was to make their feet appear narrower in order to give the impression that they never put enough weight on them to make them spread. It is the same vanity that made foot-binding fashionable with ancient Chinese women who preferred that people thought they were carried everywhere they went; or modern women who sport ultra-long fingernails lest anyone would think they were typists.

But they were entitled to an occasional bit of vanity. They lived and worked in a no-man's land that was widely known as "The Great American Desert," and generally regarded as unfit for habitation of any kind. They proved the perception wrong and established patterns that hundreds still live by.

Charlie Goodnight, the Texas rancher, paid them a touching tribute when he wrote:

"I wish I could find words to express the trueness, the bravery, the hardihood, the sense of honor, their loyalty to their trust and to each other. They kept their places around a herd under all circumstances and if they had to fight, they were always ready. Timid men were not among them... the life did not fit them. I wish I could convey in language the feeling of companionship we had for one another. Despite all that has been said of him, the old-time cowboy is the most misunderstood man on earth. May the flowers prosper on his grave and ever bloom, for I can only salute him... in silence."

But, as has happened often, Charlie's feeling of nostalgia was probably misplaced. Though a great many modern cowboys are apt to do their fence riding in a pickup truck and search for strays in a helicopter; the lullabye the steers hear might be sung by Willie Nelson, and a home on the range might have central heating, not all the old-time cowboys are pushing up daisies.

Take Don Hofman of Conchos, New Mexico, for instance. He's manager of the Bell Ranch, a combination of four different outfits. He gets from one to the other in a four-wheel drive vehicle and keeps in touch with the men who work with him by two-way radio. The four or five cowboys and the foreman who keep each unit running earn a good bit more than their predecessors, about $600 a month, and the grub they get is at least more imaginative. Their bunkhouses are more comfortable, too, but the way they go about their job hasn't changed much. The dust is just as dusty, the mud just as slippery as it was a century ago. The cattle they round up are bigger, but so are their horses.

The pictures on the following pages, all the work of photographer Claude Poulet, were taken at four different ranches, including the Bell Ranch, where cowboys still stick to the old ways. Some are permanent employees, others move from ranch to ranch finding seasonal work, a few weeks' pay, and all the freedom that made the job so alluring in the first place. In these pages, you'll also visit the OL Ranch at Sheridan, Wyoming, a family spread, run by Fred Kussel; the CO Bar Ranch near Flagstaff, Arizona, owned by the Babitts, one of Arizona's pioneer families, and managed by Bill Lowell; and the Padlock Ranch based at Ranchester, Wyoming, and spilling over into Montana, run by Dan Scott.

None of these men works far from centers of what we call civilization, but each of them is grateful for the distance.

Facing page: Kenneth, one of the hands at the CO Bar Ranch, probably wouldn't have looked any different if he had been riding the Arizona Range in the 19th century, except for the sunglasses, of course.

Previous pages: "Where never is heard a discouraging word..." Who wouldn't be happy with a home on the range like the NC Ranch at Ranchester, Wyoming? These pages: The men who work the cattle and care for the horses at the CO Bar Ranch earn every cent of their pay and then some. But none of them would trade places with anyone who works in town. And their children wouldn't have it any other way, either. The young man twirling the lariat is the son of the ranch's manager.

Previous pages: if they think there's safety in numbers, these steers don't understand the cowboys who have gathered them here at Bear Creek, Montana, to be branded with the mark of the Padlock Ranch. These pages: ropers bring calves into the corral where the work of marking them is done by crews of rastlers. One roper keeps two crews supplied with all the work they can handle. The work is done and the calves back with their mothers almost before they realize they've been roped. Overleaf: the Montana mountains haven't seen much change since cowboys first appeared in the valleys. But what would those early cowpokes have thought about the idea of heating branding irons over a gas fire? The ones who had to ride all over the range looking for wood would probably stand up and cheer.

These pages: at the Padlock Ranch, branding calves is only one of the jobs that needs to be done. The horses need care, of course, and sick steers need to be helped. But it's invigorating work and cowboys like Greg Locke come back to the ranch at sunset ready for some hot food and a warm bunk. Overleaf: in addition to brands, cattle are also given earmarks which are easier to spot in a herd where critters don't often show more of themselves than their heads.

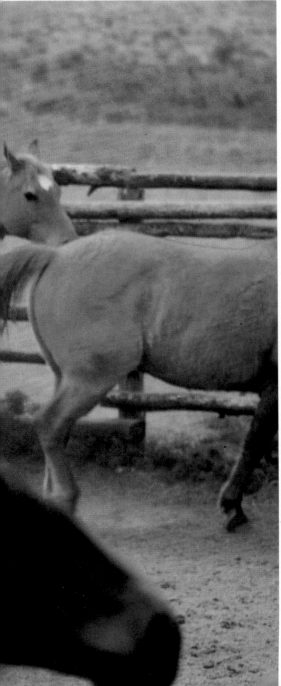

Previous pages: if you like picnics, you'd love being a cowboy at the Padlock Ranch. The trailer (bottom left) carries horses, which the hands have picked, out to the job, which is why Jim Iacolucci is standing in the midst of all those horses. These pages: looking out (facing page) over the Montana range is Dale Hermanson, who once broke two bones in an accident and had to ride 30 miles of that range to get help. Overleaf: the Padlock Ranch has a herd of about 100 horses, which are rounded up each night to give the men a good selection for the next day's work.

Though most of them get the day off, the horses (previous pages) like their jobs as much as the cowboys and they are eager to get going at roundup time. These pages: at a small ranch like the OL at Sheridan, Wyoming, branding time is an occasion for all the friends and family to pitch in and get the job done. Everybody works, but nobody doesn't enjoy it.

Previous pages: which way are they going? That's what Padlock's Cleve Redding would like to know. It isn't easy to get a herd all thinking the same. If it were, we wouldn't need many cowboys. These pages: they brand about 300 calves a day at the Padlock Ranch, one every 30 seconds. The job is done by hands like (clockwise from right) Dale Hermanson, George Eckman (and friend) and Greg Locke. Overleaf: on roundups like this one in Montana, cowhands are often in the saddle as many as 18 hours a day and will cover as many as 80 miles in a day's work.

Previous pages: that's Greg Locke hiding under the Jolan hat (bottom left). The face behind the glasses belongs to Hank Love. They're both taking hard-earned breaks from Padlock's roundup at Bear Creek, Montana. These pages: ordinarily, the Montana range is a quiet place, but roundup time more than makes up for the rest of the year. Bawling calves, shouting cowboys and the distress of the calves' mothers can be escaped if you get elected to go out and repair some fences. Overleaf: at branding time in the 1980s, as everywhere else in the West, there is an extra added attraction that would have amazed an 1880s cowboy. Calves are vaccinated at the same time. The technique of roping their hind legs and flipping them over by their tails, on the other hand, was proven the most efficient centuries ago.

These pages: the men who do the branding are called iron men, and vaccinating is done by a "gun man." In the old days, either term could have applied to any cowboy. Overleaf: the leather cover over Dale Hermanson's jeans came into the profession through the Spanish vaqueros who devised them to protect themselves when they had to ride into chaparral thickets. They called them *chaparreras*. We call them *chaps*.

Previous pages: though a man might burn himself if
he isn't careful with a hot branding iron, the
risk of cutting yourself as you cut a calf's ears
is just as great. The man taking notes is Fred
Kussel, Sr., manager of the OL Ranch. The rider
bringing in the steers is Bob Kusssel. These
pages: the determined man in the white hat is Dean
Davis, at work on the OL Ranch's roundup. Part of
the job on this family ranch in Wyoming is
teaching the craft to the next generation of
cowboys.

These pages: no, that's not a posse, it's Dale Hermanson, Cleve Redding, Hank Love and Greg Locke on the job at Padlock's Bear Creek roundup. That's Cleve on horseback trying to convince a stubborn steer that it can't hide in a thicket. Overleaf: the modern range horse is the product of generations of crossbreeding Spanish stock with thoroughbred saddle horses. In mountainous country like Montana, the sires were most often Percherons, which produced a larger-boned animal. In the Southwest, quarterhorse sires produced fast, durable stock.

These pages: sick cattle need to be captured for treatment if the herd is to stay healthy. But sometimes it's easier said than done on the roomy Wyoming range. Overleaf: riding the range with Cleve Redding in Big Horn, Montana, is the best way there is to find out why they call it "Big Sky Country."

Previous pages: most cowboys file their spur rowels so they're more threatening than harmful. The bunkhouse has improved some over the years, but the men inside are true to their traditions. They still chew tobacco, as Cal Clayton demonstrates, and George Eckman shares an age-old attachment with the frying pan. Hank Love, meanwhile, could step back a hundred years with his lariat and be recognized. These pages: the hands at the Bell Ranch in New Mexico carry lightweight tepees, while Don Hofman runs the place from an office decorated with a bison head. His grandson, Chet Pharies, will most likely carry the tradition into the 21st. century.

Previous pages: the grass-fed cow ponies need to be given periods of rest every few weeks, which makes it necessary for ranches to have large herds. When they are turned out, they always come back, usually in tight-knit groups of two or three who seem to have life-long friendships with one another. These pages: Don Hofman, of the Bell Ranch, like so many other ranch managers, often works harder and longer than the hands who help him. But he's lucky enough to have his three grandsons to help him keep an eye on things. Overleaf: they say that most cowboys were born in the saddle and some of them never bothered to learn to walk. Dale Hermanson has been seen on foot from time to time, but he doesn't like making a habit of it.

These pages: Fred Kussel, Jr. and his white horse are important to the smooth running of the OL Ranch. In fact, there isn't a member of the family without a job to do, and even the youngest of them does it well. Overleaf: each steer needs about 25 acres of pasture, and though there is an abundance of pastureland in Montana, part of the cowboy's job is leading them from one area to another when the grass begins to run out.

Previous pages: though every rodeo claims to be the best in the West, many fans are showing interest in the bronco-busting style of college students, whose enthusiasm usually runs high, as here, in May, 1985 at Cody, Wyoming. The faces on these pages belong to Padlock cowboys (counterclockwise from left): Ron Scott, Tom Hagwood and Cal Clayton. The men with the calf are ready for Tom to move in for a vaccination in true two-gun Western style.

Previous pages and these pages: one of the most fascinating things about a rodeo, more than roping and riding sometimes, is the faces in the audience. These people, and at least one dog, braved the cold to cheer them on at the College Rodeo at Cody. Well, *most* of them were excited. Though riding bucking broncos and brahma bulls are great rodeo traditions, one of the best tests of horsemanship is barrel-racing, an event that was originally intended for women only. Contestants ride one at a time around a course marked by large oil drums, each of which must be circled, but not tipped.
Overleaf: Don Hofman is about to surprise one of the Bell Ranch's horses with his lariat. It'll be surprised, but not shocked; it's part of a daily routine for both man and animal.

These pages: college-level rodeo competitions gave the sport a new dimension beginning in the late 1940s, when college-educated cowboys, and girls, began appearing on the scene. Overleaf: if you ever get the impression that flipping a noose around a running steer from the back of a horse who's running even faster is easy, it's probably because of cowboys like Cleve Redding, who make it *look* easy.

These pages: calf ropers in rodeos make their job look easy. But like the bronc rider, whose challenge is to stay on board for eight seconds, you know in your heart that either job is tough.

Overleaf: the audiences for branding look quite disinterested, but that's the nature of cows. Still, one can't help wondering what's going through the mind of the cow and the calf in the background watching these cowboys work.

These pages: the calves being roped and the steers being wrestled at the rodeo in Cody probably have no idea they're involved in a competition. But their instinct surely tells them there is probably a place out there in the Wyoming hills where they would rather be. Overleaf: the creamy color the Spanish called *palomino* is one of the legacies of the Spanish ponies in today's cow horses. Many often have a smoky blue color called *grulla* and a striking combination of the two called *appalusa*.

Previous pages: destroying a diseased animal and coping with an occasional rattlesnake are both part of a cowboy's daily routine, which includes chasing strays, leading steers to water and catching himself a horse for the next tour of duty. These pages: the work at the CO Bar Ranch in Arizona takes place in the shadow of snow-capped mountains not very far from the Grand Canyon. The tenderfoot at the bottom of this page is at the Bell Ranch in New Mexico. He is not making a career decision. He took care of that when he was younger! Overleaf: these steers on the Padlock Ranch's Big Horn range in Montana are a cross breed of black Angus and Hereford cattle, and are not even related to the longhorns that marched up from Texas a century ago.

Previous pages and these pages: who is that with George Eckman? It's the kind of friend any man would be pleased to have out there on the range in Montana. George Eckman lives on the range by himself year 'round. The biggest part of his job when it isn't roundup time is keeping the bulls and the cows separated, except during a two-month mating season.

Previous pages: a ranch's stock of horses, like this one at the Bell Ranch, is called a *remuda*, another cowboy word with roots in Spanish Mexico. The horses are usually trained by professionals who are cowboys, but would never dream of being involved with cows. These pages: when barbed wire first came to the West, everybody either hated it or loved it. But the ones who hated it most were cowboys who thought it was going to put them out

of a job. As it turned out, it gave them a new one. Mending fences became part of the job along with tending horses and cattle. Overleaf: there are some signs of civilization beyond the fenced-in range at Sheridan, Wyoming, but the houses are still far enough apart to make a man and his horses feel they have the whole world to themselves.

Previous pages: Frannie Locke works as hard as Greg Locke at roundup time in Big Horn, Montana. The brand on the horse's flank identifies it as the property of the Padlock Ranch. These pages: branding time is a time of hard work for every cowhand. There are critters to catch, fences to be mended and, finally, branding to be done. The cattle penned-up waiting for the final job would probably by just as happy if nobody bothered. Overleaf: back in the days when they drove cattle up from Texas to the Kansas railheads, the lines stretched for miles. These steers in Montana are a different breed, but the man on the horse is of the same breed that kept them moving in the 1870s.

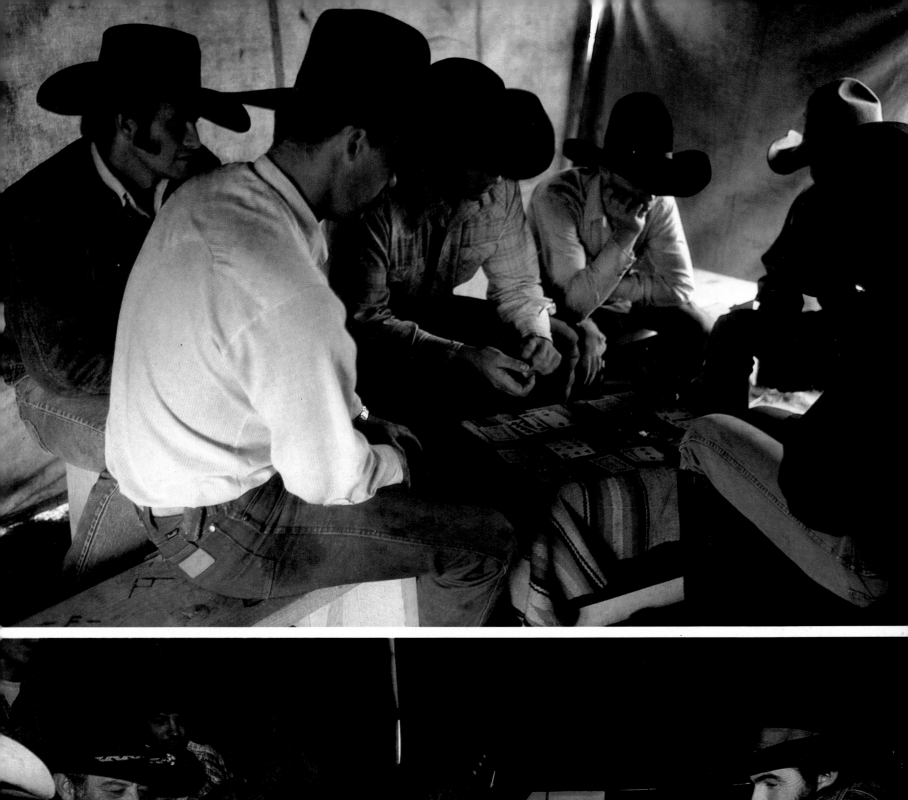
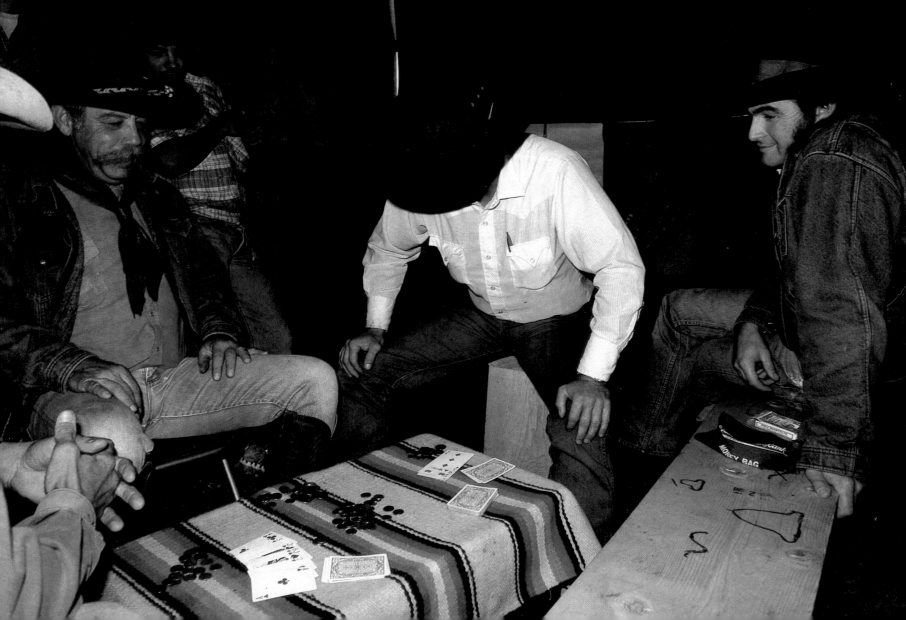

Previous pages: the forefathers of these Bell Ranch hands in New Mexico never dreamed that their descendants would sleep and pass the time in Indian-style tepees. These pages: riding the range gives a man plenty of time to think, but among the things cowboys think about most is lunch time, when they all get together at the modern-day chuck wagon, a tent pitched in a grove of trees. Overleaf: every cowboy needs to know what to do in a driving thunderstorm, and in Montana they sometimes have to contend with heavy snow. But what every cowboy gets in abundance is dust. It's everywhere on a cattle drive.

Previous pages: is there any place Cal Clayton would rather be than on the back of a good horse in Bear Creek, Montana? If there is, he doesn't mention it very often. These pages: after having been rounded up, the horses at the Bell Ranch do their best to look their best for the cowboys who, meanwhile, are down at the Post Office, which happens to be part of the ranch. At least one is still out to lunch, and others are getting in some roping practice.

Previous pages: at the CO Bar Ranch in Arizona, the cattle don't have their horns cut as they do in many other places. Not only does this allow them to protect themselves, but the horns make it easier to rope them. These pages: the Padlock Ranch spreads out over so much territory that the manager uses a small plane to keep up with all the things going on in every corner, from fence-mending to herding.

Previous pages: as soon as the sun comes up, the hands at the CO Bar Ranch are riding off to start work. But the first job is to select, rope and saddle one of the fresh horses in the remuda. These pages: in spite of the snow on the mountains, the work on the range in Arizona is hot and dusty for both man and horse. But the CO Bar is one of the oldest continuously-operated ranches in the West.

These pages: Frannie and Greg Locke often work together as a team, and she sometimes helps with the cooking for the whole outfit, who keep busy roping and branding, herding horses or standing around waiting to be fed. Overleaf: there may be a bright golden haze on the meadow down in Oklahoma, but the haze is a little less romantic and not much to sing about when cattle are being driven across the Montana range.

These pages: When Tim Mulloy looks over his shoulder at the CO Bar Ranch, he sees snow-capped mountains in the distance and the sandstone San Francisco Peaks in his own front yard. Overleaf: the bunkhouse at the CO Bar Ranch isn't as luxurious as the hotels down in Scottsdale, but it's a comfortable home away from home for these Arizona cowboys, who don't hanker much for luxury anyway.

These pages: not many cowboys carry sixguns any longer, but George Eckman is one of the exceptions. It's part of his protection against rattlesnakes and other varmints. The young man on the horse is the son of cowboy Cleve Redding, waiting eagerly for the day when his feet will reach the stirrups. Overleaf: a perfect team: Dean Davis and companion at the OL Ranch in Wyoming. The horse is wearing a hackamore, made of rope and used for training or for tying up gentle horses. Dean has a regular bridle over his right arm.

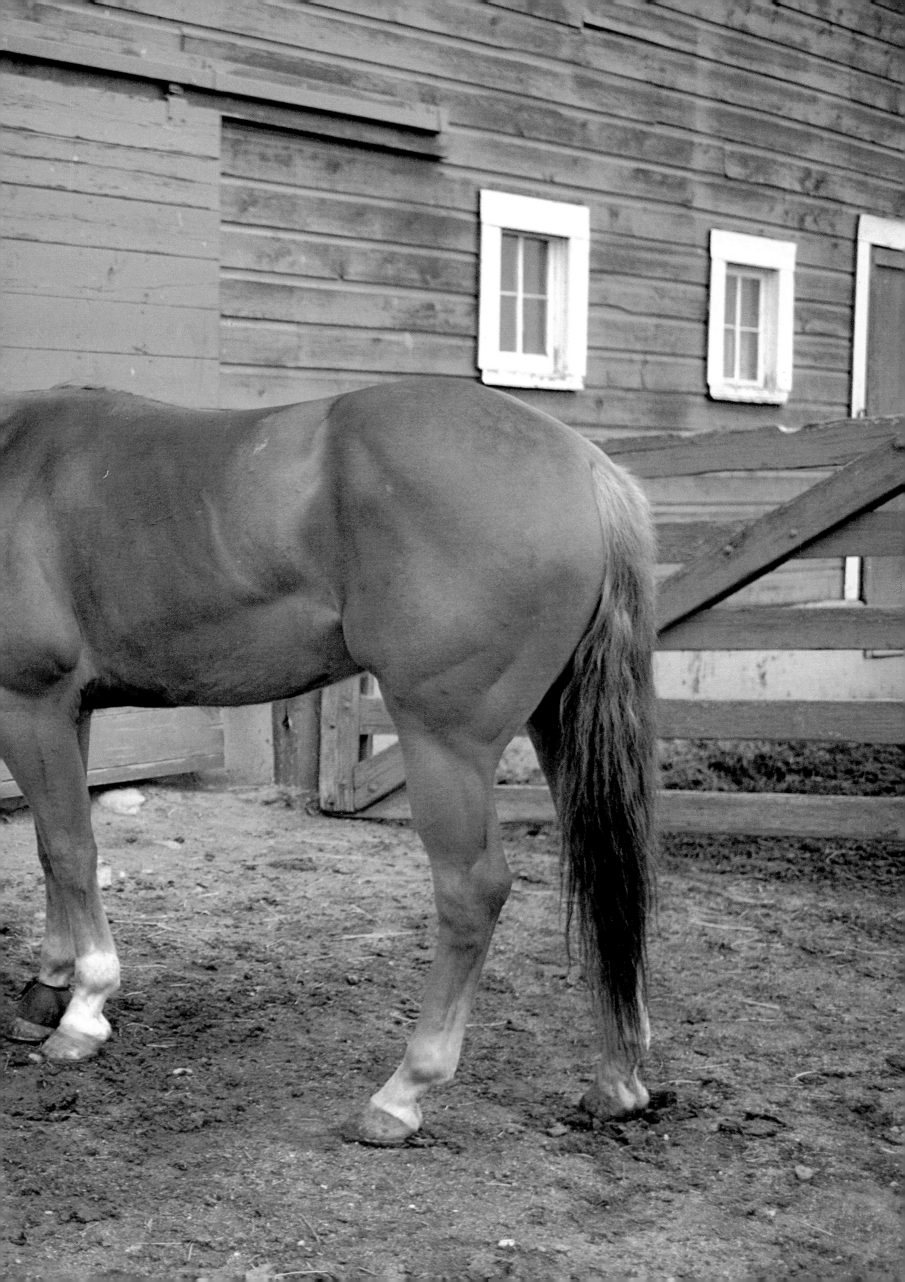

NC RANCH
REGISTERED HEREFORDS
GEORGE LEGERSKI
& SONS
OME OF
DO NO HEIR 29th

Previous pages: Dale Hermanson isn't going to use that rifle to drive intruders off the Padlock Montana properties. It is used to kill sick cattle and predators. After all, why would places as inviting as the spreads at Bear Creek and Big Horn ever turn away strangers? These pages: when cowboys go home, it's usually to the bunkhouse. But Frannie and Greg Locke have their house near the ranch, 50 miles away from the nearest town. Overleaf: when the cows come home, the cowboys are usually behind them making sure they don't stray somewhere else. In this case, it's Fred Kussel's family and men he's hired to help them at the OL Ranch.

Previous pages: before they were called
"mavericks," motherless calves in the old West
were called *dogies*. Over the years, the name was
applied to all calves who often, like the pair
left, wander away from the herd. They won't get
far, the cowboys behind them have the situation in
hand. These pages: the high point of every
cowboy's life is going into town to get duded up.
In Sheridan, Wyoming, you can get a saddle, a
lariat or a perfectly-shaped hat along with the
news of the day. Overleaf: if the beer at Sheridan
isn't flowing freely enough, drop over to Hardin,
Montana, and visit the cowboy bars there. You can
get into a friendly conversation or a game of pool
or find a furry dog to pet.

Previous pages: at the Padlock Ranch in Bear Creek,
Montana, J.C. Gupton, George Scoobe, Mike Jointer, Jim
Iaculucci and Ron Scott are down by the barn; the cow
boss, Bill Link, is out on the range (top right), and
other hands, including Cleve Redding's son, are getting
ready for work. These pages: at Sheridan, the bar
cowboys prefer is the *Mint Bar*, but the *Corner Pocket*
is the place to meet your friends when you go looking
for fun in Hardin. Overleaf: meanwhile, back at the
ranch, the horses bide their time. These days, when a
cowboy goes into town, it's usually in a pickup truck.
Following page: in Montana, a little house on the
prairie is usually part of a setting that makes you
want to stay there forever.